GO FORWARD

TURNING TRIALS INTO TRIUMPH

PATRICK KARIUKI

TRILOGY
PROFESSIONAL PUBLISHING MEETS POWERFUL PROMOTION

A wholly owned subsidiary of TBN

Go Forward
Trilogy Christian Publishers A Wholly Owned Subsidiary of Trinity
Broadcasting Network
2442 Michelle Drive Tustin, CA 92780

Manufactured in the United States of America
10 9 8 7 6 5 4 3 2 1
Library of Congress Cataloging-in-Publication Data is available.
ISBN: 979-8-88738-601-0
E-ISBN: 979-8-88738-602-7

ACKNOWLEDGMENTS

First and foremost, to my Lord and Savior Jesus Christ for grace and providence to go forward daily.

To my confidant, best friend, and wife, Miriam. Your moral support and encouragement have kept me growing and going forward.

To my easy-going and perceptive son, Bill, and my sharp-witted and vivacious daughter, Jill. You are the reason I gained the great title, Dad.

To my fellow believers at Renewal Springs Church in Dallas, Texas. Your support and faithfulness are one of the reasons I keep going forward.

Special thanks to Rhonda Webb from Trilogy for professional advice and correspondence through the production process.

I am grateful to WorldMissionsMedia for valuable help in editing, as well as Amanda King for working on the design of this book.

I am indebted to many others at Trilogy Publishing who worked diligently and handed my tardiness with grace.

God bless you all.

DEDICATION

Affectionately dedicated to three precious people whose inspiration fuels my desire to *go forward*: my sweet wife and best friend, Miriam, and our precious kids, Bill and Jill.

TABLE OF CONTENTS

PREFACE

Imagine trying to drive a car whose rear-view mirror was larger than the windshield. Imagine running a race where the main rule was that you had to spend more time looking behind than looking ahead. Imagine meeting someone whose eyes were at the back of his head. These scenarios sound incredulous and may even be outright ridiculous, yet they perfectly illustrate the very life that many people live. Many people are unable to fully grasp the opportunities of the present and future because they are so encumbered by the burdens of yesterday. The past may be a good tutor but not a good master. The road ahead no doubt requires greater attention than the road already behind. Solomon, an ancient and wise king, said that the day of death was better than the day of birth (Ecclesiastes 7:1).

The rear-view mirror gives us perspective while driving, but we only glance at it while our gaze is fixed on the windshield. Yesterday, with all its blessings and lessons, will give us perspective and maybe inspiration, but our focus must be on today and tomorrow. This book is a peek into the Word of God and life to find the wisdom, the justification, and the road map to break free from the fetters of your past and reach forward to all that God has for you. This book is a practical tool to aid you in disentangling from the chains of yesterday. The need to keep going forward, as basic and straightforward as it may seem, is a very vital life lesson. God designed your legs to run faster while moving forward than moving backward. Do not listen to the insidious lies of Satan that you cannot go forward, that your past will always define you. You can and will go forward.

The battle to *go forward*, to refuse to get stuck in the past, is a daily battle. The most eminent personalities fight this battle daily, and the least among us must fight this battle daily. You are fighting this battle, and let us all admit it is one tough battle. The scene may change frequently and abruptly, just like in a movie, but the storyline is the same. The enemy is working hard every day to keep you from becoming the best version of yourself. We also sabotage ourselves by co-operating with the enemy or by embracing self-defeating habits long enough for these habits to ultimately shape our character and, ultimately, our destiny. Apostle Paul, clothed with God's wisdom and personal experience, summed it up best:

> *Brethren, I do not count myself to have apprehended; but one thing I do, forgetting those things which are behind and reaching forward to those things which are ahead, I press toward the goal for the prize of the upward call of God in Christ Jesus.*
>
> **Philippians 3:13–14**

Go forward!

SECTION ONE

GO FORWARD

CHAPTER ONE

FLAMES IN THE SKY

The huge flames of fire danced high in the sky, illuminating the dark night all around as the hungry fire consumed every inch of what had been a magnificent family home. We stood about five miles away, sobbing and holding each other's hands for comfort and support. The day was August 19, in the year 1993. Our only crime on that Thursday night was to belong to a tribe that was in political competition with another tribe. We were huddled together with many villagers in a school, watching as bright fires illuminated the dark African night as our home was reduced to rubble. Our home was big and grand, and now marauding warriors had burnt it to the ground. We heard from reliable sources months later how they had first broken the door and ransacked the whole house, looking for anyone inside to kill. We had left the house a few hours earlier.

My dad, fueled by sheer adrenaline and raw masculine

rage, had matched courageously in the night, accompanied by a few men, to confront these raiders and fight them. God, in His mercy and providence, made sure the two groups did not meet that night. He came back to where we were camping in the wee hours of the night and confirmed that several houses in our homestead had been burnt. Molo area in what is now Nakuru County in Kenya was the epicenter of politically instigated tribal clashes. My family, by village standards, had been well off, but now we were staring at a very uncertain future. My parents, now rendered homeless and with five school-going children, did not know where to start. Their hard toil and sacrifice of many years had gone up in smoke on one cold Thursday night. Where do you begin, and how do you even think of *going forward*?

The aftermath of this unfortunate incident was an exceedingly difficult season for my family, as well as many others who went through even worse harrowing experiences. Many people lost loved ones and properties, and many fled, never to return. I was in high school then, and now my family was crammed in a very tiny two-roomed house in the school compound where my dad was a teacher. My brother and I shared a ridiculously small one-room a quarter mile away. This very humble place, as humiliating and depressing as it was, became our home for the next eight years. My mother had a serious nervous breakdown that threatened her very life, two of my siblings were sent to stay with a relative, and the rest of us adjusted to very downsized living quarters, which would have been the equivalent of where we would have housed servants who tendered our land. How do you pick yourself from that and *go forward*?

This afternoon, as I type away and write this page, I am writing in my home office in a spacious house in a great North Texas suburb while my parents are asleep halfway across the world in their own permanent three-bedroom stone house in a spacious compound with their car parked outside. My mother's depression was completely and indeed miraculously healed, and our former house is but a distant memory in our collective psyche. God can and will hold your hand and lead you out of the wilderness you find yourself in if you will let Him. I cannot pretend to prescribe an exact roadmap that He will use or give you a perfect prescription or remedy, but I join the writer of Proverbs in urging you to "trust in the LORD with all your heart, and lean not on your own understanding; in all your ways acknowledge Him, and He shall direct your paths" (Proverbs 3:5–6).

Why Do You Cry to Me?

Does God really want us to go forward in life, or is He just neutral, leaving us to our own devices? A scripture in the Book of Exodus answers this question with clarity and precision, but first, the background for context. The children of Israel had been in slavery in the land of Egypt for four hundred and thirty years. Pharaoh and His people in Egypt had unleashed a reign of terror and brutality on these hapless Israelites, and they heaved daily under the cruel and heavy burden of slavery. God finally sent a deliverer named Moses to prepare the whole nation of Israel to escape the heavy chains of oppression. Pharaoh, buoyed by his subordinates and unwilling to relinquish all the free labor the children of Israel were providing, dug His heels and refused to let them go.

God was in no mood to negotiate with Pharaoh and used His servant Moses to unleash judgments over Egypt. The ensuing tug of war between Moses and Pharaoh results in devastating plagues, and finally, Pharaoh bows to the power of Moses' God. The jubilant Jewish population, with all their wealth and gold from Egypt, matched out of Pharaoh's hand to the land God had promised their forefathers. This spectacle must have been something to behold, so spectacular the best movie directors of Hollywood cannot adequately recreate. Pharaoh swiftly changed his mind and decided to pursue this great population, so they could come back and serve His country, as they had done for four hundred and thirty years. Imagine the scenario, a great population, numbering at least two million, with livestock, gold, jewelry, and all the wealth they could carry, and then they encounter the sea. Their promised land is beyond a sea they cannot swim across; there are no boats to carry two million across, they are surrounded by mountains to the left and right, and all the soldiers of Egypt are speeding toward them to drive them back to slavery!

I do not know what was going on in the mind of Moses, especially because many were murmuring and complaining, some suggesting it would have been better to remain in Egypt. Moses cries to God as pandemonium and anarchy spread in the camp, "And the LORD said to Moses, 'Why do you cry to Me? Tell the children of Israel to go forward'" (Exodus 14:15). Now, please tell me how that makes sense. Going to the left, right, or even back would make sense, but going forward did not make sense. Walking on water was not one ability endowed on people, so just what did God mean by telling the people to go forward when the very toes of their feet were on the edge of a massive sea?

66

God's instructions require more than just our five senses. We need a sixth sense called faith.

What really is faith? Faith is simply hearing a word from God and then both believing it and acting on it. "So then faith *comes* by hearing, and hearing by the word of God" (Romans 10:17). Moses then clears his throat and announces, "Ladies and gentlemen, the break is over; gather your belongings; we are going forward!" Talk of leadership crisis!

Do you know God will never ask you to retreat and surrender just because the way forward is difficult or the battle is fierce? God will never ask you to quit the fight of faith and go back to the world. God did not tell Moses and His people to take the practical and pragmatic solution of negotiating with Pharaoh to return to Egypt under better working conditions. Faith sometimes goes beyond the natural, the practical, or the pragmatic. Going forward in your life will often mean stepping out beyond the rational and practical and reaching out your hand to a hand that is bigger and stronger than yours. God may be giving you instructions that do not make sense to you because His instructions make "Godsense." The devil's instructions are always nonsense, but God's instructions are called Godsense (I just made that word up, do not search it up). Listen to how Godsense sounds like: "'For My thoughts *are* not your thoughts, nor *are* your ways My ways,' says the LORD. 'For *as* the heavens are higher than the earth, so are My ways higher than your ways, and My thoughts than your thoughts'" (Isaiah 55:8–9).

The way that leads to life is narrow and has many hurdles and struggles, but God will never ask you to change lanes and merge with the traffic on the big wide road that leads to destruction. God has no pleasure in those who forsake the narrow road just because there is pressure and difficulty. "Now the just shall live by faith; but if *anyone* draws back, my soul has no pleasure in him" (Hebrews 10:38). The children of Israel obeyed that difficult command, and God literally made a highway in the middle of the sea, and the entire population literally walked on the dry ground, with the waters of the sea providing a gigantic wall to the right and to the left. The whole story is recorded in the Book of Exodus, chapter 14. What sea of impossibility are you facing today? What crisis is keeping you awake at night? Listen carefully for God's instructions through prayer and reading the Bible, and when He speaks to you, just go forward!

Men of Ephraim

We are in a raging battle against the flesh, the world, and the devil, yet retreat is neither a wise option nor a safe strategy. You are most vulnerable when you are running away from the devil. Crowns are given after the battle is won, and trophies are handed at the finishing line of a race, not the beginning. The children of Ephraim prepared for battle, matched confidently to the battle line, and then listened to the formal accusation they received from the Psalmist, "The children of Ephraim, *being* armed *and* carrying bows, turned back in the day of battle" (Psalm 78:9). Imagine all the preparation, training, and the pep talk. Imagine strong, able-bodied men, kissing anxious brides and crying children, armed to the teeth, and bound by duty and love for country matching across hills and ridges and upon facing the enemy soldiers just trooped back to their wives. That is shameful.

The believer in Ephesus 6:10–18 is instructed to put on the whole armor of God. This believer has the whole body covered and protected except the back, meaning the moment he turns back to flee, he has the back exposed. Your only safety while fleeing is to outrun the enemy's arrows, and if you want to try that, good luck with that! Satan cannot resist the urge to shoot fiery darts at fleeing believers, so do not show him your back. The scriptures indeed admonish us to "resist the devil and he will flee" (James 4:7). Make the devil the one to flee; otherwise, if you are the one fleeing, your back will always be hurting from the enemy's darts. No wonder so many Christians have back trouble.

Imagine the regret and the shame the men of Ephraim had to live with, the taunting from their enemies they had to endure for running away without shooting even a single arrow. Many people have surrendered even without a fight, and the enemy continues to take surrendered territory without even fighting for it.

Why should the enemy keep finding uncontested territory in your life while you keep retreating and boxing your life into a small and meaningless life?

The character of the enemy is not such that he can see how much you have suffered and leave you alone. The enemy is described as one "who made the world as a wilderness and destroyed its cities, *who* did not open the house of his prisoners" (Isaiah 14:17).

Yesterday's Victories

Faith is a now phenomenon. Today's battles cannot be fought with yesterday's faith. You can draw some motivation and encouragement from past victories, but you should not camp there. Do not build a monument where you were just supposed to pitch a temporary tent. Many believers and yet-to-be believers tell riveting stories about their faith and other adventures of their past but are currently doing nothing. Today's hunger cannot be cured by the food you ate yesterday. The children of Israel were instructed to collect enough manna to last them a single day, except the day prior to the sabbath when they would collect a double portion in order to rest on the sabbath day. The Lord wanted them to trust Him daily, and He provided to them, one day at a time, for forty years. God did not provide them giant refrigerators and coolers to store up manna. They ate fresh manna, hot from heaven's kitchen on a daily basis.

Yesterday's victories do not exempt you from fighting today! Yesterday's failures do not disqualify you from fighting today. God wants you to go forward, to keep the fire of your passion burning, to learn from yesterday but not be stuck in it. God commanded Moses to instruct Aaron, the High Priest, that the fire of the burnt offering was not to go out. "A fire shall always be burning on the altar; it shall never go out" (Leviticus 6:13). Maybe you are stuck because your past is very shameful because of mistakes you made. Rahab was well known in the city of Jericho, according to the second chapter of the Book of Joshua, but not because of making or selling girl scout cookies. It is worth noting even the king knew her house, and she did not sing in the choir. The scriptures say she was a prostitute. She is, however, the only one, together with her family, that escaped alive when the city was destroyed. She rose from this sordid life, made peace with God, moved with the children of Israel, and eventually became one of the five women named in the family tree of Jesus Christ in the Book of Matthew 1:5. What a comeback! What is your excuse? The heroes of faith, which is really the "faith hall of fame" in Hebrews 11, lists men and women whose great faith we are encouraged to emulate. Rahab, the seducing, husband-snatching sister, is named in the same breath as Abraham, David, and Moses as a hero of faith. Curiously, of the five women named in the Book of Matthew in the genealogy of Jesus, only Mary, the mother of Jesus, could pass a background check. The others had some issues. Tamar slept with her father-in-law, Ruth was a widow, and Bathsheba married King David after the king killed her husband. These stories do not make a great resume, yet these precious ladies learned how to go forward. Will you go forward?

The Scriptures remind us that "we have this treasure in earthen vessels, that the excellence of the power may be of God and not of us" (2 Corinthians 4:7). Noticed the irony? "Treasure" means "great value," but then it is stored in vessels made of dirt, meaning little value. Why would God not put these great treasures in golden vessels or at least silver vessels? Remember Godsense? Yes, it does not make human sense, but it makes perfect Godsense.

Go Forward Testimony

I will call her Carol, for that was her real name. I could tell her cute hands were trembling slightly, and the shifting in her seat was a giveaway that the conversation was uncomfortable for her. I tried to wear a cool demeanor, but I was almost sure a thin line of unwelcome sweat was running down my back. How was I to convince this beautiful girl that our lives were meant to be intertwined in a way closer than just mere friendship? "When I look at my future as a father, husband, preacher, or whatever responsibilities life bestows on me, I just see it alongside you," I volunteered. As far as I could judge beauty, no girl in the University of Nairobi could hold a candle to Carol. "I don't expect you to be armed with an answer right away, but if par adventure you have it, can we please hear it?" "Please give me time to pray," she requested. Back then, at least in my culture, we did not propose on one knee with a ring at hand. I felt a bit relieved. She asked to pray, and I had already prayed. I figured out the answer would be a big teary "Yes." The writer of Proverbs 31:10 asked, "Who can find a virtuous wife? For her worth *is* far above rubies." Well, I had found her right in the halls of

Hall 12, Main Campus, University of Nairobi, or had I?

Four months later, after a dose of humility, I met Carol again. She had been on the long break students took after two semesters. We met in her room on a Friday. I had graduated about two months earlier. She asked me to come the next day, and I was the happiest man in Nairobi the next day in the morning as we walked down State House Road to Central Park, adjacent to Uhuru Park. Let me cut to the chase; the answer, delivered and served with a gentle godly smile, was, "No, I think it is not you." I quoted every verse I knew about relationships and marriage, and Carol, in her humble signature smile, requested we revisit the issue three years later after she finished her course. I knew it was over; we said our goodbyes, and I dragged my feet to the bus stop to go to Dandora, where I was staying at the time. I am writing this twenty-two years later, and I am sure Carol is fine, wherever the good Lord led her.

One year later, armed with more wisdom and humility, I sat across the table and said to the stunning girl looking at me, "Miriam, when are you intending to get married?" "Why?" she asked shyly. "Because I intend to play a very vital role in your wedding." She looked at me and asked, "Do you want to be the best man, Patrick?" "No," I replied quickly. "I want to be the one putting on the ring!" Dead silence. Like Carol, she asked for time to pray. Oh Lord, not again! Funny that I would dread prayers, having been the prayer secretary in the Christian union while I was a student. Two and a half months later, my phone rang in the office where I worked, and the voice on the other end said, "I have prayed and decided it's Patrick." She said yes, and after a year and a half, she walked down the aisle at International Christian Center in Nairobi to become my wife, and, as I type this in my home office, sitting next to my college-going son, Miriam and I are looking forward to celebrating twenty-one years of a wonderful marriage.

Oh, I forgot to mention that a few months before I proposed to Miriam, I was praying one Saturday morning in a big church in Dandora phase 2, I think it was called All Nations Church, when God spoke to my heart these words, "It's Mburu's sister." Godfrey Mburu is one of Miriam's older brothers. There were two sisters, Miriam, and Alice, who could fit that bill. I knew both of them pretty well. God, in an unexpected way, made me aware of which of the two He had in mind. They say hindsight is 20/20, and looking back, I can say Miriam is the best thing, apart from receiving Jesus Christ, that has ever happened or will ever happen to me. My whole family loves her dearly, especially my parents. I struck gold, a virtuous Proverbs 31 woman!

CHAPTER TWO

WELCOME FIRSTBORN, GOODBYE JOB

I was shaking and breathing heavily as I approached him to request a few days' extension to pay my rent. He was well known in Ruaka, the sleepy suburb ten miles east of Nairobi, where my wife and I had settled after our wedding. The landlord was as mean as a rattlesnake and had as violent a temper as a man could have. He particularly disliked Christians, and when I lost my job without a salary in the last three months, I did not know where to turn. My wife had a job that paid so little I cannot even write the amount here. We had just become husband and wife less than six months prior, and we had already finished the little savings I had from my previous job. The landlord was very crude and mannerless in getting his rent. He made it his business to announce, very loudly for the neighborhood to hear, that you were late in paying rent, and the ultimatums and threats were laid out for all to hear.

We were kicked out of this two-bedroom apartment, and we found refuge in a very tiny one-room that was barely the size of our kitchen in the previous apartment. My wife's sister was paying the rent for this tiny room, which she had vacated for us, and had moved to live with her friend in the same block. Employment was hard to come by, and between looking for jobs, I would spend entire days inside Karura Forest praying and fasting. I was super excited when I met a man who promised to employ me as a manager in his enterprise. I had met the man months earlier in my former job, and after we secured an office, hired a secretary, and worked for a month, the man simply disappeared into thin air. I had never met him since and had no clue if he was dead or alive. He conveniently was unavailable when my first salary was due, and that ended what I had thought was a promising job.

The next job I got was enjoyable, and I began to like it until I asked for permission to attend a religious festival-cum-training in the Northern town of Garissa. The boss curiously informed me she would call me back to inform me when to come back to work. The call has never come back. I had been fired very courteously, and just when I thought life was getting too tough, my wife informed me she was pregnant with our firstborn. I did not know whether to laugh or cry. I did not know why I was experiencing these kinds of hardships when it came to my career. I recall about two years earlier being interviewed for a big job with an international organization, and after the interview, the recruiter casually informed me that I had done well in the interview but was too young to manage the salary! This corporate snob was staring at me and telling me that I had passed the interview, but she was sparing me from destroying myself with the fat check. Talk of rubbing salt to injury! Navigating the slippery path of job hunting in Nairobi in those days was a tough challenge, but I kept going forward, hanging in there with bulldog tenacity.

Do not hesitate to start going forward today just because you do not have all your ducks lined up. You do not wait for all the lights to turn green before you drive out of the house. I wish I could say that I never encountered any more challenges and setbacks in my working life, yet I can say that every single time I put my trust in God in spite of prevailing circumstances, God came through. Going forward requires both the inspiration or motivation and the skillset. The first part of this book is meant to inspire, motivate, and challenge you to keep going forward. This is meant for your heart. The second part of this book is meant to equip and give you the necessary tools to go forward. This is meant for your head.

*An inspired heart and an educated head
are the perfect prescription
for going forward.*

This book is both a software and hardware for your next level of growth.

Why Are You Sitting Down?

There is an interesting story in the Bible, in the Book of 1 Kings 13, of a young prophet from Judah who was sent by God to deliver a message to King Jeroboam at Bethel. The prophet was given firm instructions not to eat bread, drink water or return to Judah the same way he had gone. The young prophet saddled his donkey and set out to deliver God's message to King Jeroboam. The kingdom of Israel had divided after the death of King Solomon, with Rehoboam, son of Solomon, reigning in the South (Judah) and Jeroboam reigning in the North (Israel). The temple King Solomon built was in the South, in Jerusalem. King Jeroboam, afraid that the northern tribes might troop to Jerusalem to worship and become loyal to the king of Judah, made shrines in Bethel and Dan. The young prophet from Judah was sent to prophesy against this altar in Bethel that King Jeroboam had erected. The message was effectively delivered and spectacularly confirmed by the splitting of the altar King Jeroboam had erected.

King Jeroboam, attempting to intimidate the prophet, had his hand withered, only getting respite after the prophet prayed for him.

The story of the young prophet, however, ends in great tragedy after he disobeys the clear instruction of the Lord to go forward after his mission. He sat under an oak tree to rest, probably basking under the success of this successful ministry. The news of this young prophet must have spread in Bethel like wildfire. The *Bethel Daily News* was already doing a special edition on this dazzling young preacher from Judah, and maybe a journalist or two were on his trail to secure a special interview. The resting prophet was unaware that at the very moment he was resting, another old prophet was cruising at high speed to bring him back to the city. The old prophet represents the past. The old prophet is a picture of where God used to be, not necessarily where He is. The old prophet eventually caught up with the resting young preacher and instantly announced his credentials, saying, "I too *am* a prophet as you *are*" (1 Kings 13:18).

The only thing the old prophet still had was his past reputation. He was keen to flash that in the face of the young prophet. I wonder why God had to send the young prophet from Judah while the old resident prophet in Bethel was available. The old prophet lied to his younger colleague that God had instructed him to take the young prophet back to Bethel for dinner. Why did the old prophet lie to the young prophet? Why did he so desperately want the young man to go back with him? The old prophet probably wanted some legitimacy in his ministry, a kind of endorsement from the young prophet. I wonder why God had instructed the young prophet not to linger around Bethel or even eat and drink anything in this land. God was probably trying to save this young prophet from the poisonous ministry of the old prophet. The past, however glorious, may sometimes be dangerous to cling to.

The past is sometimes very sneaky, seeking to hijack the present and assassinate the future.

The young prophet was detoured for simply refusing to go forward. He was sitting under an oak tree when he was supposed to be riding home to his destiny. Do not let your past success dazzle you so much that you camp at the monuments of your past accomplishments. The young prophet returned to the home of the old prophet and, a few hours later, while finally on his way home, was mauled to death by a lion. Do not let the glory of the past blind you from the responsibilities of today and tomorrow.

Elijah, Eat and Go Forward!

The Book of 1 Kings chapter 19 has a very fascinating story of Elijah the prophet. The nation of Israel had deserted the worship and service of the one true God, turning aside to serve Baal, the Canaanite god of fertility. Elijah confronts this situation head-on, first declaring a three-and-a-half-year moratorium on rain and later killing all the prophets of Baal after a power contest on Mount Carmel. Jezebel, the wife of King Ahab, was the patron of the Baal prophets in the land, and after she heard the report of their killing, she swore to kill Elijah. Victory and mountaintop breakthroughs do not always cushion us from difficult moments later, and the discouraged prophet decided to run for dear life. He lay down under a tree, tired and discouraged, wising his earthly assignment would end there and then.

> *Then as he lay and slept under a broom tree, suddenly an angel touched him, and said to him, 'Arise and eat.' Then he looked, and there by his head was a cake baked on coals, and a jar of water. So he ate and drank, and lay down again. And the angel of the LORD came back the second time, and touched him, and said, 'Arise and eat, because the journey is too great for you.'*
>
> **1 Kings 19:5–7**

Elijah was ready to give up. He had called fire from heaven, killed the prophets of Baal, and literally restored the nation to the worship of the one true God, but he lay down on a tree, too discouraged to do anything. God dispatched an angel to feed and encourage this gallant soldier who was now too discouraged to go forward. A two-course meal of cake and water was all it took, and the prophet was commissioned for the next assignment. Elijah walks, on the strength of that meal, for forty days and nights to Horeb, where he has another wonderful encounter with God. Going forward is for those who have failed miserably and those who have succeeded spectacularly. No one is exempt. Your past failures or successes should not impede or stop you from going forward.

Peter and Judas

None of the twelve apostles of Jesus was perfect. None of them had an impressive resume, and if Jesus had engaged an employment bureau to search, interview, and recruit, probably only Judas would have sailed through. Peter, the loudest of them all, denied Jesus three times, cursing in the process and swearing he did not even know Jesus. Judas, on the other hand, betrayed Jesus, handing Him over to those who would eventually crucify Him. These two men let Jesus down in a big way. Peter, however, allowed Jesus to restore him and was ready to go forward despite his great failure and heeded the instruction of Christ to "feed My sheep" (John 21:17). Peter did not get stuck in his mistakes and failures. Running to God, even after we fail, is the way to God. Do not run away from Him, like Cain did after killing his brother Abel. "Then Cain went out from the presence of the LORD and dwelt in the land of Nod on the east of Eden" (Genesis 4:16).

Judas, on the other hand, was too stubborn or proud to humble himself, seek forgiveness and go forward. He opted to take the way of defeat, and he checked out by way of suicide. He was proud that he had failed but could not bring himself to seek forgiveness. Forgiveness and grace are found on the way home to the father, as the prodigal son discovered. The prodigal son did not find grace running away from home but running home. Determine today that you will be like Peter, not like Judas. *Go forward!*

Go Forward Testimony

I think my days at the University of Nairobi were a real spiritual boot camp for me. God used difficult circumstances, especially financial difficulties, to equip me with vital lessons on faith and trust. I experienced many financial miracles, as I will recount at the end of every chapter in the *Go Forward Testimony* section. I was in my second year and was residing in Hall 9. I was running very low on finances, as I had only received a partial amount of the government's loan, thirty thousand Kenyan shillings instead of the maximum forty-two thousand shillings. I had not received any bursary, so it was just a matter of time before I completely had no money left. Finally, the dreaded day came, and I had just enough money to buy a packet of rice. The pay-as-you-eat system that had been introduced was quite expensive, and so most students were cooking in their rooms, using some cheap electric stoves. I walked to Uchumi Supermarket on University Way and bought a packet of rice.

I decided to cook right away and poured some of the

rice on my table to remove any chaff. God is my witness; when I was pouring the rice, a ten-shilling coin fell from inside the rice packet. The packet of rice had been sealed; I am the one who opened it, and how a ten-shilling coin was there, I cannot tell. I ran to a nearby student shop outside the hall and bought two eggs. The next time I was pouring rice, another ten-shilling coin fell out. Funny how I always poured rice very carefully, keenly watching if more money would fall out, but it never happened again. God was not giving me a formula; He was teaching me a principle. I have never experienced anything like that since, nor had it ever happened before. What are the odds that one packet of rice would contain two ten-shilling coins, which would end up in the hands of a hungry student who needed the exact amount to buy some eggs? God then miraculously provided money through a relative to provide for me for the rest of the semester.

CHAPTER THREE

THREE WEEKS OF HIGH DRAMA, THEN GRACE

High school was a nightmare for me. I was noticeably young and small and neither energetic nor athletic. Bullying was rampant, and most high schools were boarding schools, meaning we spent three months in school before we could break for the holidays. Our school was a mixed school, and having both boys and girls in that setting presented its own set of challenges. One issue that made my high school experience so daunting was the theft of mattresses. Allow me to explain. Upon reporting as first-year high school students, we were given a mattress, among other things, which was meant to serve one for the duration of four years of high school. The school system then operated on a term basis, and each year had three terms. Dinner time was always around 6:30 p.m., after which we went for evening study time from 7:00 p.m. to 9:00 p.m.

A bizarre and extremely annoying, and incidentally frequent incident was to go to the dormitory and find your mattress stolen by another student. The ritual of going from bed to bed trying to identify your stolen mattress was cumbersome and dangerous since a much stronger guy could be sleeping on it. Our school had two dormitories for boys, which housed about three hundred boys in total. My mattress was stolen at least fifty times in the four years, and at some point, I think even the blankets, effectively rendering me a "homeless" student. High school at the time was just a voluntary glorified jail. One night, my mattress was stolen, and so I decided to steal another student's mattress. I was in junior high, which was then referred to as form three. I did not know I had stolen the mattress of the school captain, and after a search was done, the mattress was found on my bed.

Dramatic Hitchhiking around the Country

I was roughed up by the boys, and though I sustained no serious injuries, I was very embarrassed by the incident. Mob justice in Kenya is rampant, from schools to the streets in urban dwellings and in rural areas. The retrogressive culture of shaming, beating, and often killing offenders and suspected offenders was and is still prevalent, which is a sign of a nation with a sick soul. I was so embarrassed, and when everyone was asleep, I packed a few belongings and escaped from school at dawn. I jumped over the school fence, hitch-hiked for miles, and paid a fare to a town called Nyahururu, after which I traveled to the capital city, Nairobi. I had no money, I was only seventeen years old, and my parents had no idea I was not in school. A school term was usually three months, and as a boarding student, it meant you spent the three months without going home for the holidays. I spent a few hours in Nairobi's Uhuru Park, and in the evening, I hopped into a bus going to an estate called Jerusalem.

My seventeen-year-old brain reasoned that a place called Jerusalem, a name in the Bible, must surely be a safe place. I alighted before I got there, and after a few hours of getting into buses randomly, not knowing where I was going, I finally arrived at a sprawling slum called Kawangware. I was sleeping at the bus stop when I was awoken by a skinny poor looking man, probably in his fifties, who demanded to know what I was doing alone at midnight in that risky place. I gave a rehearsed sob story, with concocted details of how I had gotten lost trying to locate a relative. The man offered me a place to spend the night, and I ate dinner in his little one-roomed house. He had only one bed and invited me to sleep on the edge while he slept on the other edge. I could not fall asleep, and I could tell he was not asleep either. Late in the night, the man who had seemed so understanding and friendly wanted sex. I told him no, promising to consider his request the following day. He snored into the night, leaving early in the morning. I woke up at around eight in the morning, and I knew I had to escape. I could not dare to stay in this house with a stranger and was afraid to stay there. I ransacked his house, searching for money to steal, but found none. The thought of burning his house down and escaping came to mind, but I decided it was not a wise idea. How dare this scoundrel demand such an unnatural and godless thing of a seventeen-year-old?

Encounter with Two Uncouth Men

I boarded bus number 46, if my memory serves me right, and was back in town. God, in His mercy, had let me escape unharmed from the jaws of a predator. I cannot recall all the events of my escapades that afternoon, but I do recall I ended up in an estate called Umoja. I arrived in Umoja hours after trying in vain to trace my uncles, who were truck drivers in an estate called Dandora. My escapades at the time could provide a Hollywood screenwriter with enough material to produce an edge-of-your-seat thriller. I was accommodated by a mini-bus driver for the night, who also bought me meat for dinner. God bless you, sir, wherever you are. I had narrated to him how I had gotten lost trying to locate my uncles to report my grandmother's death. My grandmothers were, of course, alive and well, but there was no way the man could verify my claims in the pre-cellphone era.

I was able to travel from Nairobi the following day to Nakuru, where drama awaited me. An old man, probably in his sixties, offered to buy my dinner in a restaurant, which was located near what was then the Nakuru railway station ticket office and customer's lounge. The man then disowned the agreement when we were halfway through dinner, insisting I had indeed promised to buy the meal for both of us. I ate quickly as his few teeth chewed slowly and carefully and, without notice or warning, dashed out of the hotel at supersonic speed. He tried to follow me but was intercepted by a waiter and forced to pay for our meals. He caught up with me half an hour later, but he quickly sensed I was ready and willing to knock off the few remaining teeth in his mouth. I was really becoming wary of these older men in their fifties and sixties. The train lounge was for bona fide travelers only, and police patrolled the place to keep away pickpockets and petty thieves. I was rudely awakened by a policeman who demanded what I was doing, to which I retorted that I was waiting for the train just like the other passengers.

The Unplanned Train Ride

The policeman asked for my ticket, and I marched to the counter and bought a seven-shillings ticket to a nearby town called Njoro. The train finally arrived around midnight, and I hopped in like all the others. I just did this to escape harassment from the police officer. The train arrived in Njoro, but I could not alight at such a late hour, so I just pretended to be asleep. I was awakened rudely by a ticket inspector an hour later who demanded why I did not alight an hour earlier when the train arrived at Njoro. I tearfully narrated that I had accidentally overslept and that my only relatives lived in Kisumu, a city almost one hundred miles away. I arrived in Kisumu early in the morning and was amazed at how hot, humid, and stuffy the town felt. I made up my mind I would not spend the night in the town and went to the bus stop with my made-up story of why I did not have bus fare but had to travel urgently to Nakuru. I told my story for several hours to different bus crews, and eventually, one bus driver offered to help. I was back in Nakuru at the railway station that night, where I spent the night juggling between dodging the police and trying to pick pockets of sleeping travelers. I did not manage to steal anything, and I concluded I was not gifted and brave enough for this line of business. The following day I hopped into yet another bus, this time to a little town called Gilgil, famous for hosting military barracks. I had a relative who lived in the town, and I arrived hungry and weary. I was looking quite haggard after almost a week of country-wide tours punctuated by high drama and weird old men.

The man worked in a butchery in the shopping center and rented a tiny one-roomed apartment, and he sent me to his home, about two miles from where a casual laborer lived alone. The man was nicknamed "Mtalii," which is Swahili for "tourist." I do not really know whether it was poverty or ignorance or just sheer adventure, but Mtalii lived a strange life. First, Mtalii had only one pair of trousers, a black one. He would wear it from Monday to Saturday and wash it at night, ready for Sunday. Mtalii's earthly possessions, all his wealth in this world, were kept in a sack. The wealth was three or four shirts, a jacket, a few underwear, and very few utensils; that was it. The man was however strong, very happy, and without a care in the world. I would call this home for the next two weeks, adapting to the lifestyle of Mtalii and beginning to think of a career as a shepherd boy. I was done with school and the hassle of stealing mattresses and all that stuff that made school a living nightmare.

Encountering Grace

My dad, in the meantime, had gotten word that I had disappeared from school. He went to school and confirmed the news, and embarked on finding his missing son. First stop, Gilgil! I was having what I called lunch, but it was really the most pathetic little meal a poor, starving, and jobless teenager could be able to put together. I heard a knock on the door, and when the door opened, my dad walked in. I almost fainted. He looked at what I was eating, and tears rolled down his cheeks. He did not scold me, rebuke me, or even seek an explanation. He wanted us to go home. I did not get time to bid goodbye to Mtalii, and we left and went home. My dad encouraged me to go back to school, urging and helping me overcome the shame and embarrassment of the incident that had led me to run away from school. He treated me like the biblical father treated the prodigal son in Luke 15. I was back to school in a few days, and after one year of studying and stealing a mattress when mine was stolen, I finished high school without another incident. The system was such that one could repeat the final high school year to get better grades, and that is what I did. I repeated my final high school year but in a different school and qualified to join the University of Nairobi.

Today, I am a holder of a master's degree from a top American seminary. I had run away from school and prepared myself to start my career as a shepherd. God had a better plan for my life and used my dad to encourage and urge me forward. I walked back to the same school I hated and had been mistreated. I decided to go forward. I decided that I would not let adversity and shame become the final chapters of the story of my life. I decided that a few jeers or mocking from fellow students could not be reason enough for me to sabotage my life by quitting school prematurely when my parents were working hard to give my siblings and me a decent education. I do not know your story. My ordeal lasted only three weeks, yours could have lasted thirty years, but you can still rise, and against all odds, *go forward*. The prodigal son in Luke 15 discovered that there is always grace on your way back home. No one helped him when he was running away from his father, but when he chose to return, despite the shame and the loss he had caused his father, he found mercy, favor, and love. Make the decision in your mind and make the first practical baby step to go forward and watch how God will begin to connect the dots and the missing link. *Go forward!*

Let Go of the Hugs of Pity

---------------🍺---------------

Many people are languishing in the prison of self-pity. They hang on to the pain of difficult experiences and have unconsciously fallen in love with the pain because of the pity and sympathy it generates.

They have become addicted to the attention and consolation these experiences evoke, not to mention the hugs and encouragement these may bring. Jesus healed a paralyzed man and told him to take his bed and walk, not lie on it. The hurt and the pain may have been real, and time may not heal all wounds, but God, indeed, does heal broken wounds. "He heals the brokenhearted and binds up their wounds" (Psalm 147:3).

Go Forward Testimony

First-year students in any institution have their unique way of adapting to school life. My unique way of handling finances was to carry all the money I had in my wallet wherever I went. One day I was waiting for a sociology class to begin outside what was called the multi-purpose hall (MPH). I dozed off, and when I woke up, the class was underway, so I rushed to class, unaware I had left my wallet behind. I did not notice I had dropped my wallet where I had dozed off outside MPH. I had two thousand three hundred shillings in the wallet, with the two thousand shillings in an inner compartment in the wallet. I then prayed this funny prayer, "Lord, whoever finds this wallet, let him steal the three hundred and leave the two thousand shillings in the inner part intact. Let the three hundred be the cost of my own carelessness, in Jesus' name."

I was residing in Hall 5, like many male first-year students, and as I strolled back, I saw a group of students holding a school ID and scrutinizing all who came in. One of them, who was not a believer, was waving the two thousand shillings in his hand, and when I walked in, he pointed at me. He had recognized me from the student ID. Someone had found the wallet outside MPH, stole the three hundred, and dropped the wallet in Hall 5 with two thousand shillings inside. The gentleman that found the wallet with two thousand shillings waved at me when I entered our hall of residence. I learned to believe my own prayers. Lack of faith cost me three hundred shillings, which was a lot of money then.

CHAPTER FOUR
FAVOR-FILLED TRIP TO ISRAEL

I was driving on Beltline Road in Dallas, Texas, one Saturday afternoon when I drove past Baruch Hashem synagogue. I had driven past this synagogue many times before, but that day I had a strange thought to go inside and give a small offering to help a poor family in Israel. I had fifty dollars in my wallet, so I drove inside and gave the money to the gentleman who met me at the door. I did not get to meet the rabbi. I was feeling embarrassed to walk into the synagogue with such a small amount of money and give it to support a family in Israel, but I believed somehow God had directed me to do that. I gave the money, and the gentleman was very gracious, and soon I was driving on and forgot the incident. Strangely, I sensed some peace about the incident, though the donation amount was small.

I had always desired to visit the land of Israel and have

always loved the Jewish people and their land. I understand the Jewish roots of the Christian faith, remembering that "to them were committed the oracles of God" (Romans 3:2). I have always understood, as a gentile believer, that I was a wild branch grafted into the olive tree, and the Jewish people are the natural branches.

For if you were cut out of the olive tree which is wild by nature, and were grafted contrary to nature into a cultivated olive tree, how much more will these, who are natural branches, be grafted into their own olive tree?

Romans 11:24

I had always desired to see the land of the Bible and believed that God would one day open a door for me to visit the holy land. An opportunity to visit finally came about in 2016 when the ministry of Promise Keepers sponsored me to visit the holy land with a group of pastors from all over the country. The trip was to cost about four thousand dollars, but my out-of-pocket expenses amounted to about a thousand dollars.

I made all the necessary preparations, and the day of the trip finally came. I flew to Los Angeles, excited that I was on my way to Israel finally. We lined up, and our passports were being inspected as we chit-chatted with excitement. I was suddenly taken aback when the airline officer at the desk inquired about my visa, and I responded that I had been told all along that I did not need a visa to travel to Israel. I was traveling with a Kenyan passport, and the ministry official I had been dealing with had assumed all along that I had an American passport since I was already in America. I could not travel to Israel without a visa, and I watched in utter shock as all the other pastors, more than a hundred of them, were cleared and disappeared behind airport doors to board the plane to Tel Aviv. I felt crushed and disappointed, and after a few frantic calls, I was informed that there was an Israel consulate in Los Angeles.

Living in Goshen

I took a cab and went to the embassy. I had no appointment, and the security officer refused to allow me to proceed upstairs to the consulate without an appointment. I understood this was standard protocol, but I also understood divine protocol sometimes overrules human protocol. I dialed the consulate number, and when someone picked up the phone, I said, "Sir, my case is very special and very urgent. I need to speak to someone face to face, please." I explained my case, and graciously I was allowed to present my case face to face. I presented my case, informing the interviewing officer that I was part of a pastors' delegation that had already flown to Israel. My trip was fully sponsored, and the airline ticket had already been purchased. The officer listened intently and gave me several forms to fill out, and I was asked to come back the next day in the morning. I spent that afternoon making many phone calls and faxing documents to the consulate that were required to assist in my visa application. Two different incidents happened that evening that were unique. The first incident was when I decided to take a stroll in the evening from my hotel room near the consulate. I was walking down the street when I noticed the name of that street was *Goshen*. I immediately remembered that Goshen was the place the children of Israel were residing when the ten plagues were ravaging the nation of Egypt. The land of Goshen is where Joseph, as Prime Minister of Egypt, had settled his family when they had fled from the drought in Canaan. You can live in your own prophetic Goshen. You can be in a state of peace and tranquility even when surrounded by chaos and turmoil all around!

My heart was immediately flooded with supernatural peace. I knew God was giving me a prophetic picture that I would experience favor and peace, and my case would have divine favor attached to it. I began to worship, lifting up my hands and speaking in tongues. I was in Goshen. My case would be settled in a supernatural way by a supernatural God! I was back in my room, and after I slept, I woke up with a strong desire to worship. I began to pray, sing, and raise my hands in the dark, sitting on my bed. Suddenly, I began to shake almost uncontrollably. Tears began to flow freely, and I could feel waves of heat flowing through my body. I cannot adequately use words to describe the experience, but I knew a deep sense of peace in my heart. I dosed off eventually and woke up early in the morning to go to the consulate and find out what my fate was. I was finally ushered in, and in less than thirty minutes, I was out of the place, visa at hand. I called the trip organizer, and in about thirty minutes, I was rebooked for the next flight, which was leaving for Tel Aviv in less than three hours. I hailed a cab, got to the airport, and checked in. I was not even subjected to a lot of searching and was escorted like a VIP to the plane, and in no time, I was airborne en route to Tel Aviv, Israel.

I deplaned in Tel Aviv and was met by a gentleman who had my name prominently displayed on a huge placard and was transported all the way to the Tiberias by the Sea of Galilee, where I met my colleagues. I cannot prove it, but I have always believed that my small fifty-dollar offering in a synagogue somehow had a connection with my miraculous and favor-filled trip to Israel. First, I paid only a thousand dollars for that trip, while the others paid four thousand dollars. Secondly, I was granted an emergency visa, and my case was taken up first, though I had failed to do due diligence before the trip. I was rebooked for a flight that was leaving in hours and escorted to the plane like royalty. I proceeded to have a great and memorable trip to Israel, fulfilling a desire I had carried in my heart for many years.

Many times, we are paralyzed by fear and are unable or unwilling to take a step of faith when we are faced with impossible deadlines. What do you do when there is so much to do yet so little time to do it? What do you do when the task is so huge, yet the resources are so few? What do you do when you feel so ill-equipped or unprepared for the task? How could I even hope to apply for a visa and join my fellow pastors for a trip that was only nine days? How do you go forward when every piece of evidence around you shows the trip is over? How do you just take a sling and five small stones and run towards a towering giant, armed and experienced, for a fight? How do you run forward when it is much safer and more pragmatic to run away?

David Moved Forward

King David is no doubt one of the most colorful and admirable characters in the Old Testament. The charismatic king of Israel was a multi-talented man whose heart-stopping victories and escapades would make great Hollywood movies. David wore many hats and was at home soothing the soul of troubled King Saul with anointed music just as he was running forward to fight a great giant twice his age and height. David, a man after God's heart, was a great worshipper and the sweet Psalmist of Israel, yet in a time of weakness, we read of him planning the death of his own soldier to cover up for his adulterous liaison with the soldier's wife. He oscillated between spiritual mountaintops and depressing valleys. Reading the Book of Psalms captures David swinging between these two ends of the spiritual continuum. David succeeded wildly in many instances but also failed miserably in others. David, however, learned to *go forward*, refusing to be imprisoned by both his failures and his successes. Three specific incidents from his life bring out this strength of going forward very vividly.

The first incident is David's confrontation with Goliath, the philistine giant, at the valley of Elah. Goliath was not an ordinary soldier whose only claim to fame was his great height. Goliath was a towering and intimidating killing machine whose very appearance on the battleground made the soldiers of Israel retreat and tremble in dread. He had sought a soldier to fight with, and for forty days, no one, even on a suicide mission, dared to accept this challenge. Goliath presented himself twice a day and repeatedly declared, "I defy the armies of Israel this day; give me a man, that we may fight together" (1 Samuel 17:10). Well, he could not get a man, but God had a boy who could answer that challenge. He had zero military experience, but his resume showed that he was a shepherd boy. The boy, only a teenager, declared he would face the giant, and when the laughter died down, they tried to drill sense into the handsome-looking lad, carefully explaining who Goliath really was. David was dressed in King Saul's armor, but it was too huge and heavy for him. He could not use any of their weapons, so he finally settled for a slingshot and five smooth stones.

Goliath looked at David and probably wondered, *Wow, this boy is so much smaller than me!* David, on the other hand, could have wondered, *Wow, this giant is so much smaller than my God!* The armies of Israel and Philistia fixed their eyes on these two unlikely contestants, and while they watched, something very unprecedented happened, catching both camps by surprise. The scriptures record that "David hurried and ran toward the army to meet the Philistine" (1 Samuel 17:48). David went forward. He did not just take a defensive position; he went on the offensive. He ignored the fact of his inexperience, the disapproval of his elder brother, and the scorn of experienced soldiers to run forward! The army of Israel had been planning and strategizing for forty days and had been paralyzed by analysis. You cannot plan forever, and after all the planning, you will still need to go forward eventually.

David was ready to stand out rather than just fit in. He was ready to stand when the spotlight was on him and when there was no support from his corner. He was ready to play without home-court advantage.

You will not always find a willing partner or group to go forward with. David did not find a single soldier who was willing to go forward with him. Going forward can be a lonely journey sometimes. The warmth, security, and comfort of a crowd can be very alluring; after all, there is safety in numbers, right? You cannot go forward until you are ready to step out alone. You must be willing to go forward without crowd approval. The Scriptures give a sad commentary of religious leaders in ancient Israel that were convicted by the Gospel message yet could not confess Jesus and follow Him openly because they were addicted to the praise of men.

> *Nevertheless even among the rulers many believed in Him, but because of the Pharisees they did not confess Him, lest they should be put out of the synagogue; for they loved the praise of men more than the praise of God.*
>
> **John 12:42–43**

These men were so approval-hungry that they sacrificed the eternal at the altar of personal aggrandizement. You cannot go forward if your chief motivation is Facebook likes!

Ziklag Was Burning

The second incident from the life of David happened a few years later before David became the king of Israel. David had gained such notoriety after killing Goliath that women sang and danced, saying, "Saul has slain his thousands, and David his ten thousands" (1 Samuel 18:7). King Saul approved neither the lyrics nor the dancing, and so he decided to put this little party to an end permanently, by doing to David what David did to Goliath. David understood that he was anointed to fight Goliath, not to fight Saul, and so he left town hurriedly. This is an extremely important lesson on going forward. You are not anointed to fight every battle that comes your way. You fight Goliath, but you escape from Saul. King Saul was anointed to lead Israel. He was a deeply flawed man, but the oil of God was on his head, and so Saul was God's problem, not David's problem. David had opportunities to kill Saul, but he did not. Pick your battles wisely, and let God deal with His own anointed. They may be flawed and not measure up to your expectations, but you are not anointed to fight them.

David escaped and received political asylum in the land of the Philistines, ruled by Achish. David became loyal to King Achish and even led his men to raid the southern parts of Judah several times. One day there was war between Israel and the Philistines, and so David gathered his men to help his gracious host against the land of Israel from which he had defected. The Philistine commanders were, however, suspicious of David's intentions, arguing that there was a danger of David defecting back to Israel and helping King Saul slaughter the Philistines. The Philistine commanders' fears were obviously legitimate, though David was genuinely willing to fight against Israel. David was turned away and went back to his asylum city of Ziklag, but there was a problem! I will let Prophet Samuel tell the problem in his own inspired words:

> *Now it happened, when David and his men came to Ziklag, on the third day, that the Amalekites had invaded the South and Ziklag, attacked Ziklag and burned it with fire, and had taken captive the women and those who were there, from small to great; they did not kill anyone, but carried them away and went their way. So, David and his men came to the*

city, and there it was, burned with fire; and
their wives, their sons, and their daughters
had been taken captive. Then David and the
people who were with him lifted up their
voices and wept, until they had no more power
to weep. And David's two wives, Ahinoam the
Jezreelitess, and Abigail the widow of Nabal
the Carmelite, had been taken captive. Now
David was greatly distressed, for the people
spoke of stoning him, because the soul of all
the people was grieved, every man for his sons
and his daughters. But David strengthened
himself in the LORD his God.

1 Samuel 30:1–6

The city of Ziklag had received unwelcome guests
while David was away, David's house was burnt down,
and his family was kidnapped. The men who were
David's friends now held stones in their hands, ready
to kill him. David had been rejected by the Philistine
commanders, and now his own compatriots were ready
to kill him. His family had been kidnapped, and he was
homeless, sitting dejected next to the smoldering ruins of
what was his house. How do you go forward from that?
David, however, strengthened himself in the Lord, his
God. David's secret to success was neither his talents
nor his courage but his relationship with his God. David
wiped his teary eyes and asked the Lord, "Shall I pursue
this troop? Shall I overtake them?" (1 Samuel 30:8). In
other words, David was seeking God's permission to go

forward. He had every reason to just sit down dejected and defeated, as many would in the circumstances. He did not appoint a tragedy evaluation committee to assess the damage and give recommendations. He did not ask for a vote on the way forward. He prayed and asked God if he could go forward! An important principle here is that your matching orders should always come from the Lord. Pray, listen, and then go forward. "Whatever He says to you, do *it*" (John 2:5). David pursued the raiding party and recovered everything, that is, the people and the properties.

David did not wait to get strong enough to pursue the raiders. He did not wait until he was no longer discouraged. He did not wait until he "felt faith rising up."

Faith is not something we have but something we do. Faith is an action, not a feeling. You do not have faith until you attempt to do something.

Learning from Failure

The third episode, which highlights how David always moved forward, is rather a sad chapter in his life. He was by then the king of Israel, and the Lord had blessed him in many ways. David was taking a walk on the roof of the palace as his soldiers were away on the battlefield when he saw a woman bathing. He inquired who she was, and upon learning that her husband was away from home on the battlefield, David sent for her and committed adultery with her. The woman, Bathsheba, later sent word to David that she was pregnant, and he quickly devised a cover-up plan. He sent for Uriah from the battlefield, treating him to a royal banquet and wine, hoping he would go home and sleep with his wife. The patriotic man, however, slept at the door of the king's house, refusing to sleep in the embrace of his wife while his fellow soldiers camped on the battleground. His exact words were,

> *The ark and Israel and Judah are dwelling*
> *in tents, and my lord Joab and the servants*
> *of my lord are encamped in the open fields.*
> *Shall I go to my house to eat and drink, and*
> *to lie with my wife? As you live, and as your*
> *soul lives, I will not do this thing.*
>
> **2 Samuel 11:11**

David knew that a pregnancy could not be hidden for long, so he connived with Joab, the commander of the army, to have Uriah placed in a vulnerable frontline position where he could not escape. The plan works, and Uriah is killed in battle. David gives Bathsheba a few days to mourn and afterward brings her to the palace, and she becomes his wife. The Scriptures do not give us a hint on whether Bathsheba was an innocent victim or a willing accomplice. David's double sin of adultery and murder goes unnoticed in the land but not in the court of heaven. Nathan, the prophet, is dispatched to face David and announce the punishment. The child David fathered would die, and more severe punishment followed. David prayed earnestly that the child would not die and even fasted for seven days, but the child still died. David's action after the death of his son is a great lesson on going forward.

When David saw that his servants were whispering, David perceived that the child was dead. Therefore, David said to his servants, 'Is the child dead?' And they said, 'He is dead.' So David arose from the ground, washed and anointed himself, and changed his clothes; and he went into the house of the LORD and worshiped. Then he went to his own house; and when he requested, they set food before him, and he ate.

2 Samuel 12:19–20

David arose and washed himself after the child died. Remember, he had already confessed his sin and repented when Nathan, the prophet, confronted him. He had hoped God would spare the child, but that was not to be. David washed and shaved. He did not remain in a state of perpetual mourning. He discarded the mourning clothes and put back his royal robes. David then anointed himself, effectively leaving behind the stench of mourning and sweating. Isaiah 61:3 announces that God gives us the "oil of joy for mourning." David then went to the house of God and worshipped. This is very important, and

David understood to run to God and not away from God when confronted with his sin. David finally ate food to strengthen himself. David simply decided to go forward. He had failed greatly, and his sin had become public. He, however, refused to let guilt and condemnation consume him perpetually. Know when to let go. Repent and forsake the sin, then rise up, keep the mourning garments arise, and wear the robes of righteousness. Worship the Lord and then receive His strength.

David went forward to meet Goliath when he was just a teenager. David went forward as a refugee when his compatriots were considering stoning him to death. David went forward while he was king after the Bathsheba incident. He learned to go forward at every stage of his life. Going forward is not once in a lifetime event. Going forward is not even an event or a process but a lifestyle. You are not too late if you are reading this; you can go forward! Weeping may endure for a night, but the good book states that joy comes in the morning. Arise and shine, for indeed, a "righteous *man* may fall seven times and rise again, but the wicked shall fall by calamity" (Proverbs 24:16).

Go Forward Testimony

"The eyes of all look expectantly to You, and You give them their food in due season. You open Your hand and satisfy the desire of every living thing" (Psalm 145:15–16).

God is our source; He is a provider. I remember this particular day vividly. I was doing my social work degree field attachment with World Vision Kenya in a place called Soweto in Kayole estate, Nairobi. I had no money for bread that morning, and the idea of plain tea for breakfast was not very appealing. I had a hot cup of tea but no bread, so I closed my eyes and prayed a funny but sincere prayer, "Lord, You know I go without bread many times when I am fasting. Right now, I am not fasting, and I need real physical bread. Lord, I thank You for this cup of tea and the bread You will provide before I finish this cup of tea; in Jesus' name, Amen!"

I started to sip my tea and gradually reduced the pace after a few sips, afraid I would finish before the bread came. I was being assaulted by thoughts of doubt, wondering whether I was trying to push radical faith too far. I could imagine the devil whispering to me, "Do you think you will be fed by ravens like the Prophet Elijah was? You are not at that level; climb down, young man." Suddenly a fellow student, who was on attachment like me, knocked and, seeing my cup of tea, asked me, "Hi man, why are you drinking tea without bread when we have so much bread?" He dashed out before I answered and came back with two loaves of bread. My prayer was answered. He explained what happened later.

He narrated how the previous day, they had a major event where he was doing his attachment. The organization he was working with was expecting a lot of participants and had bought many crates of bread, but only a few people showed up. The students were asked to carry as many loaves as they wanted, and he had carried several. He was not a believer at the time and was not even a close friend at the time. I don't even know why he had knocked on my door at the time, except that God was answering my prayer for bread.

CHAPTER FIVE

GOD'S PROMISE TESTED

God makes promises, but more importantly, He keeps them. The date was January 1, 2001. I had graduated from the university one year earlier and was working in Nairobi, Kenya. I had organized a three-day Gospel campaign in our village and had three preachers accompanying me to the village to preach after the Christmas holidays. The response was great, and we held the final meeting on December 31, staying past midnight to usher in the new year. We congregated together on January 1, at around eleven in the morning, to pray together before leaving for the city. We held our hands to pray, and as we did, one of the preachers, a lady, suddenly began to give a prophetic utterance about my life. She said several things, which I will not enumerate here, but one thing was concerning my children. She said that my offsprings were blessed. I was dating a beautiful girl then, so this particular promise from God tickled my heart. Sixteen months from that day, Miriam and I walked down the aisle as husband and wife.

White Blood Cells versus Red Blood Cells

My son was born in November 2003, and like every father bringing his firstborn into the world, I was over the moon with excitement. I remember that Saturday afternoon vividly, for I was more anxious than my wife. I was pacing up and down the corridors of Nazareth Hospital, now in Kiambu county, and remember going to the doctor's quarters to request the attending doctor to hurry and attend to my wife. He followed me hurriedly across the field as I led him to the hospital where he worked. Never underestimate the zeal of first-time parents. Our son was born at 6:00 p.m., and the next two days were frantic with preparations to get both mother and son back home safely. I was, however, taken aback when the doctor informed me that they were not ready for discharge yet because the boy was quite sick. I cannot recall the exact medical terms or specific diagnosis, but the layman's version was that my son's red blood cells were under attack by the white blood cells.

I did not know how to pray about the issue but pray we did. I mobilized everyone I could, and we began to pray fervently for his healing. I know, medically, it may sound stupid, but I began to aggressively command the white blood cells and the red blood cells to be "at peace," "stop fighting," "behave themselves," and so on. I would go to his little crib in the intensive care unit and put my hand on his head and pray for him fervently. The nurses would be standing behind me, sometimes with teary eyes, as I repeated this routine daily. The doctor's report was not always encouraging, but intense prayer and fasting were made for the boy's recovery. I reminded God continually (not that He had forgotten) of the promise He made about my offsprings. Finally, after twenty-one days, the boy was completely healed, and we went home. Today, he is a healthy, robust young man, preparing to go to university to study sports medicine. He has enjoyed great health, and to the best of my knowledge, his white blood cells and red blood cells reconciled. To God be the glory!

Let me pause here and answer a question that many believers struggle with; why do we have to pray for something God has already promised? Do we really have a part to play in the fulfillment of a prophecy over our lives? Many would argue that we need not do anything since God's promise does not require human intervention to come to pass. Let us turn to Scripture to look at precedence and glean wisdom to help us correctly understand this important principle. The first scripture we can use to gain insight into how fulfillment of prophecy is connected to prayer is 1 Timothy 1:18, which states, "This charge I commit to you, son Timothy, according to the prophecies previously made concerning you, that by them you may wage the good warfare." From the verse above, we can make important observations. First, Timothy had received specific prophecies about his life, but Paul urges him to use that fact to wage the good warfare. Timothy could not just sit around patiently, waiting for the automatic fulfillment of the prophecies. He was rather urged to use the prophecies as gasoline for his prayer life.

Prophecy can be divided into two very broad categories. The first is what I would call "unconditional prophecy," which will be fulfilled without any human involvement. End-time events, or what scholars call "eschatological events," will be fulfilled regardless of our cooperation or lack thereof. The rapture will happen regardless, the second coming of Christ will happen, and the white throne judgment and the judgment seat of Christ will happen without our input. Many events in the calendar of God are on schedule, and they will happen at the exact time the Father has proposed. These are what we could refer to as "unconditional prophecies." The other category is what we could refer to as "conditional prophecy." Many times, in Scripture, God promises to do something if His people will act a certain way. "If My people who are called by My name will humble themselves, and pray and seek My face, and turn from their wicked ways, then I will hear from heaven, and will forgive their sin and heal their land" (2 Chronicles 7:14). This prophetic promise sounds like it is conditional to me. God's promise to hear us, forgive us, and heal our land is contingent on our calling on Him, humbling ourselves, praying, seeking, and turning away from evil.

Forty-Day Hospital Ordeal

Four and a half years later, on a cold, snowy day in Memphis, Tennessee, we welcomed our secondborn, a daughter. The beautiful girl was healthy, and we expected both mother and daughter to be discharged in two or three days. The hospital stay would, however, last an agonizing forty days. The doctors fought tirelessly to keep her blood sugar in the normal range, but she had a severe case of hypoglycemia, among other complications. Specialists were at their wit's end, and a raft of treatment options was discussed. Major surgery was on the cards, but my spirit was troubled, and I could not give consent. I prayed persistently and fasted often in that season, and one day while in prayer, I saw my daughter in a red dress on her third birthday running towards me. This, I believe, was through a gift of a word of knowledge. I had faith that my little girl would live. My wife had a somewhat similar revelation, where she saw what she understood as a demonic force oppressing our little girl through this sickness. We used these revelations from God to wage spiritual warfare continuously through prayer. Many friends and relatives were praying with us and for us at the time.

I remember one of the doctors, a young lady speaking privately to me and telling me, "At this point, it is a guessing game." I took up this issue to God in prayer, declaring that Jesus, the great Physician, was not guessing, nor was He playing a game. Finally, the breakthrough came, and guess what the problem was for the whole forty days. Apparently, she was having an allergic reaction to some particular amino acid in the milk. Special milk was recommended, and we were advised to re-introduce her to the normal milk from the grocery store when she turned one year, which we did. Today, fifteen years later, she is a vivacious, witty, and lovely girl, and she drinks a lot of milk daily! Forty days in the hospital, several specialists, and endless tests only because of a milk allergy. I learned a very important lesson. Go to the hospital and obey doctors' instructions, but let your faith be in Christ. Doctors treat, but only Jesus heals!

God had given me a specific promise about my children, but I was still required to pray and bring them up in the ways of God. Many people do not understand the prophecy and assume the promise was enough; hence they do nothing. Prophecy is God really unveiling His will and intentions for your life so that you can cooperate with God in prayer. Prophecy is not a blank check; it is a rallying call to prayer and preparation. Has God promised you wealth and riches? Well, start learning all you can about business and investments. Start being faithful in your financial dealings. Start being generous in giving to His work. Prophecy is not a call to retreat, fold arms and wait for the promise while doing nothing. Prophecy is knowing the mind of God through His revelation and beginning to do what you should so God will do only what He can.

CHAPTER FIVE: GOD'S PROMISE TESTED

I can recall moments when I was ready to give up during those trying times of my kid's hospital stays after their birth. I had to rely on the prayer and emotional support of my wife, larger family, and church to keep going forward. Going forward is not a once-and-dusted decision. Going forward is a daily decision of putting one leg after the other, even when it is difficult to do so. The battle may be so intense, the will to go on may be weak, the strength so depleted, the shame so overwhelming, and the guilt crippling, but choose to go forward!

The Merciful Father versus the Hungry Son

Jesus told a story commonly known as the parable of the prodigal son. A parable is a story that is used to illustrate an important truth. Here is part of the story, as recorded in the Book of Luke.

> *Then He said, 'A certain man had two sons. And the younger of them said to his father, 'Father, give me the portion of goods that falls to me.' So he divided to them his livelihood. And not many days after, the younger son gathered all together, journeyed to a far country, and there wasted his possessions with prodigal living.'*
>
> **Luke 15:11–13**

The young man was in a hurry to live it up, and knowing his father would not allow him to do that in his hometown, he knew he needed two things: distance and money. He wanted to be as far as he could, where no one knew him. He knew he would need a lot of money, so he came to his dad and demanded his share of the family property. Most likely, he never told his father his true intentions.

The young man quickly sold all his possessions and sneaked away. He traveled where mail could not reach him and soon became the talk of the town. He hopped from one entertainment joint to the next, with a few hangers-on that were not ashamed to help him offload the largesse. A bevy of beauties was by his side day and night, and soon he discovered that his ATM showed he had insufficient funds. The friends then disappeared faster than they had come, but luckily for him, a pig-rearing farmer could use his strength for room and board. He ate and probably slept in the pigs' sty. The young man discovered pigs were not the right company to keep, and the pig's food was not really what he wanted to feed on. Finally, he was more embarrassed to stay in this horrible place than he would be in his father's house, and he decided to go back home.

> *But when he came to himself, he said, 'How many of my father's hired servants have bread enough and to spare, and I perish with hunger! I will arise and go to my father, and will say to him, 'Father, I have sinned against heaven and before you, and I am no longer worthy to be called your son. Make me like one of your hired servants.'*
>
> **Luke 15:17–19**

Notice the young man was primarily motivated by hunger! He did not rehearse the clever little speech until he was so hungry. Hunger can make people really innovative. So, the young man set off to go back to his father's home. Emaciated, poorly clothed, and shoeless, he made the long journey home, reciting the little speech every mile. The reaction of the father when he saw his long-lost son a distance away was so moving. "But when he was still a great way off, his father saw him and had compassion, and ran and fell on his neck and kissed him" (Luke 15:20). The son was not running to meet the father; it was the father running to meet him. Imagine that. The son is walking to meet the father, but the father is sprinting as fast as his old legs can carry him! Yes, that is what happens when you walk home to the Father, our heavenly Father. He runs toward you!

You see, the son was motivated by need: the father was motivated by love. God, the Father, has always been motivated by love.

"For God so loved the world that He gave His only begotten Son, that whoever believes in Him should not perish but have everlasting life" (John 3:16).

Go Forward Testimony

I gave my heart to Christ on the second day of November, and three years later, in the university, I wanted to celebrate my third spiritual birthday but faced a small handicap, finances. I had scheduled a party in my room, in Hall 11, in the evening. I had a friend who worked in town who was going home that weekend, and I had given him a note to my dad, expecting to get some money. I dashed to his office after my last afternoon class and was all smiles as he handed me an envelope from my dad. My jaw dropped when I discovered that the envelope only contained a well-written letter from home. What was I to do, since the party was only a few hours away and I had invited several friends, about twenty of them?

I was in charge of the prayer ministry in the Christian union. I was scheduled to lead an intercessory prayer session with intercessors from 7:00 p.m. to 8:00 p.m. and then the main prayer session with the entire Christian union from 8:00 p.m. to 10:00 p.m. I was then to head straight to my room with twenty colleagues in tow, and all I had received was a letter from home saying they were doing well, and it was raining in the village. Little did I know that it was a divine setup. I had a good Christian friend and roommate called Gideon, and unknown to me, he had gone behind my back and bought everything for the party on credit. This man was the true definition of a friend; God bless you, Gideon! I was so surprised to enter my room and see the whole place so decorated, with enough snacks and refreshments as would be needed for such an event. The most pleasant surprise, however, was when they started singing happy birthday, and several sisters emerged from the opposite side of the room, my roommate's side, with a big, beautiful cake.

I have no idea, to this date, who or how the cake was made. I don't know which of them came up with the idea, and when I inquired, I was told it was a "sister's project." What a wonderful project it was, and it was such a beautiful time celebrating God's faithfulness.

CHAPTER SIX
WHY ARE WE SITTING HERE?

I have discovered I love preaching Bible stories, which is common with preachers with African heritage. I would guess maybe it has to do with the fact that storytelling was a very integral part of early childhood education and instruction in past generations in Africa. One of my favorite Bible stories is the story of the four lepers. I have preached on this passage from the Book of 2 Kings at least five times. The King of Syria, Ben-Hadad, gathered his entire army and besieged the city of Samaria. Besieging a city, which had very strong and high walls, basically meant surrounding it so that no one could enter or leave the city. The idea was to force the captured city to surrender once the food supplies they had in the city were depleted. This kind of siege would sometimes take months or even a few years. The situation became so dire in Samaria that residents began to eat their own children. The Book of 2

Kings chapter 6 records how two women ate one of the women's sons one day and conspired to eat the son of the second woman the next day—it was that desperate!

Cities could sometimes be surrounded by more than one outer wall as an added layer of protection. Samaria evidently had more than one wall since the four leprous men were separated from their brethren by a wall on the inside and from the Syrians with another wall from the outside. The four men were outside of the first wall owing to their leprous condition. Leprosy was a very traumatizing and highly contagious disease, and lepers were supposed to live far away, segregated from the healthy population. The four leprous men were therefore trapped in a sense since they could enter the gates and join their countrymen, nor could they surrender to the Syrians. They were doomed if they went in and doomed if they went out. The Scriptures do not tell us how long they endured this situation, but one day they decided enough was enough. They knew all their options pointed to a sure death, but they decided it was better to die on their feet, with wind in their face, than lie down and die on their knees. Let us eavesdrop on their go-forward conversation.

> *Now there were four leprous men at the entrance of the gate; and they said to one another, 'Why are we sitting here until we die? If we say, 'We will enter the city,' the famine is in the city, and we shall die there. And if we sit here, we die also. Now therefore, come, let us surrender to the army of the Syrians. If*

they keep us alive, we shall live; and if they kill us, we shall only die.'

2 Kings 7:3–4

Now, let us travel back in time, almost three thousand years ago, and envision these four men who were in dire straits. The four men, whose names are not even given, have been uprooted from their families and are living in isolation. They obviously are poor men since they are homeless, living outside the gates of the inner wall of Samaria. They are not supposed to have any physical contact with anyone else, not even their grandchildren. The men's food is probably dropped far away, and after the kind donor leaves, they drag their bleeding bodies to the place where the food was dropped, and they eat.

The psychological and emotional toil is probably heavier than their physical pain. They listen to the hustle and bustle of the city from behind a high wall and closed gate. They cannot join in any community celebration or event. Their birthdays were long forgotten, and their families had moved on. Lepers were so ostracized, especially because it was associated with curses and spiritual punishment, hence attracting little, if any, sympathy from the people. Jesus touching and mingling with lepers must have been so radical it must have literally been breaking news in His city. The four men must have found it even harder with the Syrians besieging the city and the resulting famine. Can you begin to imagine the excruciating anguish of hunger, depression, trauma, sickness, and so much more rolled into one? Death was so unkind to linger so long, and one day these men reached the breaking point. They decided to go look for death and put the few options on the table. Do we die sitting here, or do we die going forward? I can only speculate how long they considered and evaluated all available options, but finally, they made their decision— they were going forward!

Weak Legs, Strong Results

Now, that was the easy part; the hard part was to rise up. Can you imagine these extremely hungry, emaciated, and sickly men trying to stand on their feet? I am sure they did not just spring up like basketball players rising up from the bench to go back to the court. Standing up was a very carefully planned event, and executing it may have meant several trials and errors. Finally, they stood on their feet, stooping, and holding each other for support and, with great difficulty and pain, started making little baby steps, going to face thousands of Syrian soldiers who would only be so happy to put these miserable fellows to sleep once and for all. These eight weak and sickly legs began to march to face the army, and when they came to the Syrian camp, they could not see any soldiers around. Do you know why?

> *For the Lord had caused the army of the Syrians to hear the noise of chariots and the noise of horses—the noise of a great army; so they said to one another, 'Look, the king*

of Israel has hired against us the kings of the Hittites and the kings of the Egyptians to attack us!' Therefore they arose and fled at twilight, and left the camp intact—their tents, their horses, and their donkeys—and they fled for their lives.

2 Kings 7:6–7

Is that cool or what?

The lepers did not know what would happen apriori. They did not get a memo from the Lord the previous night that He would literally make their little steps shake the ground so much that the enemy soldiers would flee in panic. The lepers did not even know the impact their little steps were making beyond the high wall. They were just making small steps of faith, and God was multiplying the effect a million times. Listen, little steps of faith produce earthquakes of fear in the enemy's camp. "One man of you shall chase a thousand, for the LORD your God *is* He who fights for you, as He promised you" (Joshua 23:10). Going forward starts with a decision, even before connecting all the dots. Can you imagine if the lepers had sat down to plan and strategize to make sure they had a fail-proof plan before taking the first step? It is noteworthy that as long as the lepers sat at the gate, nothing happened. Their worry and discussions did not bring any miracles. God waited until they did the little they could, and then He did the much that only He could do.

God is not dependent on your strength or numbers

"for nothing restrains the LORD from saving by many or by few" (1 Samuel 14:6b). The lepers entered camp after camp, eating and drinking and looting gold. Can you imagine four people looting all the gold they could carry? The Syrians had fled in so much haste and left all their gold, weapons, clothes, and food. The story has a very happy ending. They went back into their city, Samaria, informed the king what was going on in the deserted camps of the Syrians, and the whole population came and looted the camp. The siege was broken, the famine was over, and the lepers were suddenly wealthy celebrities. I do not want to promise you that every step of faith will always have this kind of spectacular result, but I can promise you that in the larger scheme of things, you will be glad you took steps of faith to go forward.

A small smooth stone picked at random by a stream brought down a giant. A normal shepherd's staff stretched forward by faith divided the Red Sea. A donkey's jawbone in the hand of a warrior slew a thousand Philistines. A boy's lunch of five loaves of bread and two fish fed a crowd of thousands. A little is a lot when God gets in the picture.

God only gets in the picture when we go forward.

Isaiah, the prophet, said it best when He commanded, "Arise, shine; for your light has come! And the glory of the

LORD is risen upon you" (Isaiah 60:1). When we arise, the glory is released upon us. We do not produce the glory ourselves, but we will not experience His glory sitting down in despair. We must understand that in almost all circumstances, God, in His infinite wisdom, has chosen to partner with us to advance His purposes on earth. God is all-sufficient, *El-Shaddai*, and could accomplish everything without us, yet He has chosen to partner with us to accomplish His purposes here on earth.

> *This is the history of the heavens and the earth when they were created, in the day that the LORD God made the earth and the heavens, before any plant of the field was in the earth and before any herb of the field had grown. For the LORD God had not caused it to rain on the earth, and there was no man to till the ground.*

Genesis 2:4–5

I hope you did not miss it—the Lord had withheld the rain because there was no man to till the ground yet!

Prayer works pretty much the same way. God can do it without prayer, but He will not do it until you pray. Prayer is not overcoming the reluctance of God; prayer is aligning ourselves with the will of God! God is unlimited, but in a sense, we limit His influence by our prayerlessness. God has chosen to exercise His influence on earth to the extent that we invite Him in prayer. "The heaven, *even* the heavens, *are* the LORD'S; but the earth

He has given to the children of men" (Psalm 115:16). What does it practically really mean heaven is God's and the earth is ours? It means God is ruling in heaven without our prayers, and He can rule on earth as we invite Him through prayer. God has given the earth to us to rule and have dominion, and for His influence to be on earth, we have to partner with Him in prayer. That is why we pray. Prayer is the fuel that will cause you to go forward. Believers who are prayerless are literally like a car with a dead or dying battery or a car running on empty.

Elisha and the Shunammite Woman

The Book of 2 Kings records an uplifting faith-building story of a woman from a city called Shunem in the days of Elisha, the prophet.

Now, it happened one day that Elisha went to Shunem, where there was a notable woman, and she persuaded him to eat some food. So it was, as often as he passed by, he would turn in there and eat some food. And she said to her husband,

> *Look now, I know that this is a holy man of God, who passes by us regularly. Please, let us make a small upper room on the wall; and let us put a bed for him there, and a table and chair and a lampstand; so it will be, whenever he comes to us, he can turn in there.*
>
> **2 Kings 4:9–10**

The wise woman discerned that Elisha was a holy man of God and, in her wisdom, enlisted her husband's help in meeting the physical needs of Elisha by both feeding and accommodating him. The couple had no hidden motives and did not request anything from Elisha. Ministering to God's servants is noble because it honors the One who called and sent them. This couple would ultimately reap a great blessing, as we shall see shortly. Jesus taught that "he who receives a prophet in the name of a prophet shall receive a prophet's reward. And he who receives a righteous man in the name of a righteous man shall receive a righteous man's reward" (Matthew 10:41).

It so happened one day that Elisha considered the kindness of the woman and, on learning that the couple was childless, promised her that God would bless her with a child. Her act of generosity was rewarded, and in a year's time, she was nursing a baby boy. Life must have been so exciting for this couple, who had probably given up on ever raising a family, especially because the Scriptures say that her husband was old. Tragedy, however, struck as the boy suddenly died from a one-day sickness. The woman took the dead boy and placed him on Elisha's bed, the one they had made for him in the upper room. She did not even inform her husband of the boy's death nor her intentions to rush to Elisha. The woman summoned a servant, saddled a donkey, and instructed the servant, "Drive, and go forward; do not slacken the pace for me unless I tell you" (2 Kings 4:24b). I like that statement of faith: "drive, and go forward." She could have informed her husband or started crying and mourning, complaining to God, or many other things. She decided to go forward with speed, instructing the servant to break all speed limits and not slow down. I bet it was one rough ride, and within no time, that dead boy was raised back to life by Elisha. The boy sneezed seven times, and just like that, he was back in the field playing with his toys! What if the woman did not go forward? What do you think would have happened?

Elijah and the Blood Thirsty Queen

And Ahab told Jezebel all that Elijah had done, also how he had executed all the prophets with the sword. Then Jezebel sent a messenger to Elijah, saying, 'So let the gods do to me, and more also, if I do not make your life as the life of one of them by tomorrow about this time.' And when he saw that, he arose and ran for his life, and went to Beersheba, which belongs to Judah, and left his servant there. But he himself went a day's journey into the wilderness, and came and sat down under a broom tree. And he prayed that he might die, and said, 'It is enough! Now, LORD, take my life, for I am no better than my fathers!' Then as he lay and slept under a broom tree, suddenly an angel touched him, and said to him, 'Arise and eat.' Then he looked, and there by his head was a

cake baked on coals, and a jar of water. So
he ate and drank, and lay down again. And
the angel of the LORD came back the second
time, and touched him, and said, 'Arise and
eat, because the journey is too great for you.'
1 Kings 19:1–7 (emphasis mine)

Elijah had just had a great spiritual victory by bringing to a halt the worship of Baal in the land. He had enlisted the people's help to execute the prophets of Baal. God had authenticated Elijah's call by sending fire directly from heaven to consume the sacrifice Elijah had prepared. King Ahab and gone home sulking and informed his controlling wife, who had missed the party. Jezebel immediately sends a death certificate to Elisha, and the prophet skips town immediately, escaping to the desert. Elijah had just finished playing hide and seek with King Ahab for three and a half years as a severe drought ravaged the land, and he was not willing to go through another spell. Desperate, he lays down under a broom tree and prays for death. God dispatches an angel from heaven to feed the prophet and tell him to go forward. Twice the angel urges the prophet to "rise and eat." God used the angel to encourage the prophet to go forward. Elijah was afraid, tired, discouraged, hungry, and depressed, but God did not take him to heaven at that time. God instructed him to keep going forward, despite the journey ahead being too great for Elijah. Do you know Elijah did what no human being has ever done since then? Elijah walked for forty days and nights without taking another meal!

The Escaping Prophet and a Fishy Experience

There is a story that mirrors the above, but the character here has another name, Jonah. Jonah received an assignment from God, which was not what he wanted, and he decided to run away from God. He had been sent to preach in Nineveh but decided to go to Tarshish instead. The people of Nineveh were very wicked, and Jonah wanted to see them destroyed, not forgiven. Jonah had probably hoped he would have a front-row seat view as Nineveh was consumed in fire from heaven like Sodom and Gomorrah. He knew God was merciful, and so he fled to Tarshish, hoping to circumvent God's mission of preserving this great and wicked city. The ship Jonah boarded encountered violent storms, and Jonah advised the crew to throw him overboard. God had prepared a great fish, which swallowed the prophet instantly. Jonah has a three-day revival in the belly of the fish, and so you would have in the circumstances. The fish is fed up with all the movement and shouting from inside, as Jonah keeps worshiping non-stop and looks for land to deposit its human cargo. Jonah is vomited out, and I am sure if there were witnesses there, they must have repented without much persuasion. I mean, if a man lands suddenly from inside a big fish, you will want to hear what he has to say, right?

> ***Jonah arrives in Nineveh smelling fishy and in a foul mood, and the city repents to a man!***

Jonah is so discouraged that the people actually heed his message and repent, and just like Elijah, he lays down under a tree and wishes for death. God, in His mercy, encourages the discouraged prophet to go forward. The story has a happy ending for all involved!

Beware of Discouragement

The enemy will very often use discouragement as a very useful tool to derail or detour you from God's mission in your life. We have just seen how Elijah, a great spiritual giant, is overwhelmed by discouragement after a great spiritual victory. We are not immune, and we must remain ever-vigilant. Charles R. Swindoll, in his book *Swindoll's Ultimate Book of Illustrations and Quotes*, illustrates this favorite weapon of Satan thus:

> *It was advertised that the devil was going to put his tools up for sale. On the date of the sale the tools were placed for public inspection, each being marked with its sale price. There was a treacherous lot of implements. Hatred, Envy, Jealousy, Doubt, Pride, and so on. Laid apart from the rest of the pile was a harmless-looking tool, well-worn and priced very high.*

'The name of the tool?' asked one of the purchasers. 'Oh,' said the adversary, 'that's Discouragement.' 'Why have you priced it so high?' 'Because it is more useful to me than the others. I can pry open and get inside a person's heart with that one, when I cannot get near him with the other tools. Now once I get inside, I can him do what I choose. It is a badly worn tool, because I use on almost everyone since few people know it belongs to me.' The devil's price for Discouragement was so high, he never sold it. It is his major tool, and he still uses it on God's people today. (Adopted originally from John Lawrence in his book Down to Earth.)

You may not be able to walk a mile today. You may not repay all your debts in one installment. You may not lose all the weight you would want to in a month. Your journey back to health or to heal a fractured relationship may be a long, tough journey, but for mercies sake, take the first baby step. Rise up from your bed of discouragement and take one small step. Seldom is any great accomplishment achieved in one giant leap. Do you remember the four lepers at the beginning of this chapter? Make up your mind right now that you will make one small first step. Make up your mind that you will go forward. I want to believe with you, right this moment, before you proceed, that you will take the first step, the go-forward step, towards your dream and destiny. I want to agree with you in a prayer of faith that you will have the strength to make the first step to going forward in your dream. Matthew 18:19 quotes Jesus saying, "Again I say to you that if two of you agree on earth concerning anything that they ask, it will be done for them by My Father in heaven." I want to agree with you right now. Pray this prayer loud in faith, "Lord Jesus, according to Your promise in Matthew 18:19, I take the step of faith to *go forward* in_____ (fill in the blank). I arise from this moment by faith and decree that my life will never be the same again. I am *going forward*, in Your holy name, Amen."

Go Forward Testimony

I left the university campus one morning and traveled about fifty miles away for a three-day prayer and fasting retreat that was under a ministry that was called Regions Beyond Ministry. The retreat center was in a place called Ngoliba, a few miles from Thika town. The center had several small rooms where one could pray in private and a large compound if one decided to pray outside. There was a big river that flowed nearby, just at the end of the property, and this was my favorite place to go pray. I would sit on the huge rocks in the middle of the river and pray my heart out as the rough flowing waters furiously hugged my feet. One early morning, just after the sun had risen, I was praying by this river when the Lord spoke these words to my heart, "Look at the sun. It has risen faithfully every day without fail. It has been faithful and reliable, yet I am more faithful and reliable than the sun." Think about those words! I am getting emotional just re-living that moment all over again. God is more dependable and faithful than the sun! I have shared this episode because of the testimony I am about to share, which happened about two years later. I had just graduated from the university two months earlier and was sharing a small one-room apartment with an uncle in an estate called Dandora. I remember it was on the twentieth day of December, and I wanted to travel upcountry for Christmas. I prepared to leave for home, and when I got to the gate, the Lord spoke to my heart and said, "When you are gone, thugs will come and rob this apartment." I went back to the tiny apartment and looked around. I realized how poor I really was. The only precious commodity I had was a beige-colored suit that was hanging on the wall and a small radio my uncle owed. I lay my hands on the two items, the radio and the suit, and prayed another funny but sincere prayer, "My suit and radio, thugs will come after while I am gone upcountry. I command you not to leave this house under any circumstances; in Jesus' name, Amen." I closed the room and left to go upcountry. Three days later, on Christmas Eve, my uncle came home, and what a story he narrated! Thugs came, armed with crude weapons like machetes, and ordered everyone to open up. They then carried every variable thing they could, and when they reached the gates, they asked all the residents they had robbed to come and pick up their items. They said there was something about the place they couldn't understand. They did not harm anyone or steal anything. They went to another apartment immediately, where they robbed and seriously injured a resident.

Why did they not rob our place? I don't know, but this much I can say, there was a vacant room in that complex that we had been using as a place of evening prayer for a few months, and it was a place saturated with daily prayer. I believe the atmosphere was so filled with God's presence the thugs could touch nothing there. There is power in prayer!

CHAPTER SEVEN

DISCARDING MEDICINE AND RECEIVING HEALING

In the very first chapter, I narrated how our home, which consisted of a big grand four-bedroom house and several other houses in our compound, was torched during politically instigated tribal clashes. We were uprooted from our homes and spent the next nine years in a very tiny house in the school's teachers' quarters, where my dad was a teacher. My mother went into very severe depression, with constant migraine headaches and other illnesses, and was under heavy medication. Life was very tough, and everything looked bleak. Our two youngest siblings were sent to live with a wealthy relative, and my paternal grandparents relocated to another town about fifty miles away. Security was poor, and we had to be back in the school compound before dark every day. The suffering was not unique to us, as all families had been affected in one way or another. The most difficult thing, however, was to see my mother struggling with all the pain and suffering occasioned by the severe depression.

My mother was taking a few medications for her condition, and this went on for a few years. One day, she was sitting in a public service vehicle, commonly known as "matatus," in Kenya en route from the hospital, where she had been given yet another set of medications. Suddenly, as she describes it, she had an unexplained surge of faith and courage. She decided there and then that she would not take any more medications. She opened the window of the vehicle and tossed all the expensive medication she had out of the window. She instantly felt inner peace. She never experienced another bout of depression. Today, more than twenty years later, she has never had depression, and she is the happiest woman I have ever met. She just decided to *go forward* and leave depression ahead. Now, I am not saying you flush your medication down the toilet. I am just saying you can go forward! You can be healed, restored, or whatever it is you need help with. Sometimes, you need radical faith; sometimes, you need just a little faith to take a small step. You might need to continue taking your medication as prescribed, and I would highly recommend it, but you must continue believing in God for that healing. Doctors may treat, but all healing comes from God. *Go forward*, my friend.

The Good Book teaches us that "many *are* the afflictions of the righteous, but the LORD delivers him out of them all" (Psalm 34:19). We are not immune to trouble and disappointments. Our flight will sometimes encounter turbulence, but no worries, we shall have a safe landing. I wish I could tell you that after you put this book down, you will never have another difficult day, but if I did so, I would be overstepping my mandate and misleading you. I can, however, authoritatively state, on the premise of God's eternal edict, that if you put your trust completely in God, you will not be ashamed. I really do hope that no matter the setbacks, you will keep going forward, one step at a time, one decision at a time, one day at a time.

Those Who Sat in Darkness

Those who sat in darkness and in the shadow of death, bound in affliction and irons— because they rebelled against the words of God, and despised the counsel of the Most High, therefore He brought down their heart with labor; they fell down, and there was none to help. Then they cried out to the LORD in their trouble, and He saved them out of their distresses. He brought them out of darkness and the shadow of death, and broke their chains in pieces.

Psalm 107:10–14

The Psalmist describes a people that were downcast and defeated because they had rebelled against God. The people had refused God's counsel and commandments.

They perceived God's commandments as burdensome boundaries to limit their freedom. Satan often blinds our eyes, and we perceive God as a strict parent who hates it when His children are having fun. The truth, however, is quite the opposite.

God's commandments are walls of love and care, keeping us from falling over a cliff and hurting ourselves bad. God's commandments are not meant to curtail your freedom, but rather, it is a formula to really help you live a life of true freedom.

God saying no sex before or outside marriage is to keep us from the guilt, the heartache, and the burdens it will bring to us or the children who might come out of such liaisons. God is trying to help us experience the total joy the act of sex brings in the confines of marriage. Indeed, "My yoke *is* easy and My burden is light" (Matthew 11:30). Back to our verse above, so the people fell down, and there was none to help, but in their trouble, they called out to God.

Let us just unpack the message above; perhaps, we might catch a glimpse of how the Lord works to help us go forward. First, they cried out to God, and He saved them from their distress. What does it mean to be saved? What really is salvation? God saves us by reconciling us with Himself. We are born spiritually alienated from God, enemies of God. Romans 5:12 tells us that "through one man sin entered the world." We are sinners by design, and then, when we know right from wrong, we sin by decision. David says, "Behold, I was brought forth in iniquity, and in sin my mother conceived me" (Psalm 51:5). God reconciles us with Himself through Jesus Christ, His Son. God sent His Son, Jesus, to pay the penalty for our sins by dying on the cross. Jesus Christ did not sin at all, yet all our sins were put on Him as if He had actually sinned all our sins. He "bore our sins in His own body on the tree" (1 Peter 2:24). We get reconciled to God when we acknowledge this sacrifice of Jesus' death and consequently invite Him into our hearts through believing in our hearts that He died for our sins and confessing Him as Lord and Savior with our mouths (see Romans 3:23, Romans 6:23, and Romans 10:9–10).

The next thing the Lord did was to bring them out of the darkness and shadow of death. When we get saved, we have been snatched from darkness and brought into the light. The Scriptures tell us that God is light, and in Him, there is no darkness at all. "The people who walked in darkness have seen a great light; those who dwelt in the land of the shadow of death, upon them a light has shined" (Isaiah 9:2). The Lord brings us out of darkness into the light when He saves us. First Peter 2:9b reminds us that God has "called us out of darkness into His marvelous light." The verse in study above concludes that God broke their chains into pieces. Yes, God broke their chains in pieces! He did not just untie the chains like a police officer removes handcuffs from a suspect. He broke the chains into pieces. He obliterated that which held us, so we could walk in liberty. We see this pattern over and over in the Scriptures, from Genesis to Revelation. God always has our liberty in mind. God always wants us restored. God wants you to go forward. He wants to break your chains into pieces, not just remove your handcuffs. The Lord wants to set you completely free, not just have you do a plea bargain. He wants to set you free, and when He sets you free, you will be free indeed.

Compassion versus Pity

The passage at the beginning of the chapter is just one of the hundreds of passages that illustrate God's compassion. The Scriptures teach us that because of the Lord's mercy, we are not consumed. God does not just pity us; He has compassion for us. Pity is empathy, a feeling of sadness over another person's predicament. Pity is feeling sorry for another's loss. Compassion, on the other hand, is heart-deep, normally accompanied by an action to alleviate distress. Compassion compels someone to do something. Compassion is not a mere intellectual assent of an existing problem. A great story that illustrates the difference between pity and compassion is the story of the good Samaritan in Luke 10. Jesus told the story of the man who fell among thieves and was left by the roadside badly injured. A priest passed by, and when he saw the bloodied man, he passed on the other side. He probably did not want to make his white garments stained by another man's blood. The priest felt no obligation to help the man, maybe because there was no one to record his kindness. When you live for the praise of men, you cannot do anything to help without the cheering squad. Next came the Levite, and to his credit, he stopped to look. He had some pity. He was however in a hurry to attend to his ministry, and he had to keep time. How could he spoil his high reputation by showing up late and bloodied? He probably went along praying for the injured man.

Finally came along a Samaritan. He came, stopped, and helped the injured man. He bandaged his wounds and carried him to a physician to get some help. He rearranged his schedule to help this man. That is compassion. Pity does not go deep enough to make us get involved. Pity does not sacrifice and causes us inconvenience. Compassion, on the other hand, allows us to go out of our way to help. God is compassionate. He got involved in our mess. The Scriptures teach us that while we were yet sinners, Christ died for us. That is compassion! We can go forward because God's compassion moves Him to cut the chains that keep us in painful bondage.

God Does Not Have Light, He Is Light

God does not have light, He is light! Light and darkness have never had a contest. Darkness disappears at the speed of light's appearance. God is light, and He gives every person some light since we are made in the image of God. "That was the true Light which gives light to every man coming into the world" (John 1:9). We have an opportunity to let this light shine, and indeed the Scriptures command us, "Let your light so shine before men, that they may see your good works and glorify your Father in heaven" (Matthew 5:16). God is on a mission, and that mission is to move you forward. You must arise, and you must shine, for indeed, your light has come. God wants you to bask in His light, so you can reflect that light wherever you go, just as the moon reflects the light of the sun. He came to set the captives free, not just make their prisons more user-friendly. God wants you to rise up and go forward. Forgive me for repeating this thought a thousand times, but I want to deposit it in the deepest part of your spirit. Many people have believed a lie that God is indifferent about your situation or neutral about your issues. God is concerned about everything that concerns you, and if it "ain't too small for you, it ain't too small for Him."

"For I know the thoughts that I think toward you, says the LORD, thoughts of peace and not of evil, to give you a future and a hope" (Jeremiah 29:11). Yes, indeed, God is thinking about you; imagine that! God is looking at you, and He is thinking about you right now. His thoughts about you are how your future can be peaceful, hopeful, and without evil. God is thinking and strategizing how you can actually go forward. He is looking at you right now and putting down plans to help you navigate whatever stormy waters you are in right now. He sees you on the other side of this. You have to begin to see, by faith, what He is seeing. Let me show you this from the Bible, "On the same day, when evening had come, He said to them, 'Let us cross over to the other side'" (Mark 4:35). That is the beginning of a familiar story, where Jesus and His disciples encountered a severe storm in the lake of Galilee and the disciples were very afraid. Jesus, who had taken a nap, rose up and rebuked the wind and storm, bringing a great calm. How easy is it to miss Jesus' statement here, telling His disciples, "Let us go to the other side."

That is a statement of fact that Jesus made. He clearly said they were going to the other side.

The boat might fill up with water en route, you may encounter high winds and stormy waters, and your boat may sail between hippos and angry crocodiles, but if Jesus says you are coming to the other side, then you are getting to the other side!

Do you remember Prophet Jonah in stormy waters? Did he not get to the other side (Nineveh) though his mode of transportation (the belly of a fish) wasn't so comfortable? Have you read the story of Paul, the Apostle, when he was shipwrecked on his Roman voyage in Acts 27? The chapter concludes thus, "And the rest, some on boards and some on *parts* of the ship. And so it was that they all escaped safely to land" (Acts 27:44). The verses before the one quoted above show some people swimming to shore, and others described holding on to broken parts of the ship, yet all came to safety. The experiences may vary, but if Jesus said there is the other side, you would get there somehow! Can I get a Hallelujah!

Go Forward Testimony

I grew up in Kenya's Rift Valley, a place called Molo. The place was the epicenter of politically instigated tribal clashes in the early nineties. Cattle rustling was especially rampant, and we all lived in fear of cattle rustlers striking in the middle of the night to raid. One day, while on a brief visit from the university, my mother was narrating how they were living in daily fear of cattle rustlers. I read the Word of God and prayed that our cow and its calf would never be stolen. One year later, the thugs struck in the cover of darkness just as my dad was opening the door to go outside to the restroom. Those days restrooms were constructed outside, especially in the village. My dad had no idea that the compound was full of cattle rustlers armed with arrows and machetes. The thugs must have thought my dad was going out to fight them, and the second he opened the door, an arrow came flying, missing his chest by a whisker. He closed the door hurriedly, and they raised the alarm. The arrow sank so deep into the door flame. I get chills to imagine if that arrow that sank so deep into the wood had struck his chest. God spared his life and spared our cows.

CHAPTER EIGHT

STAY HERE; I AM MOVING FORWARD

And it came to pass, when the LORD was about to take up Elijah into heaven by a whirlwind, that Elijah went with Elisha from Gilgal. Then Elijah said to Elisha, 'Stay here, please, for the LORD has sent me on to Bethel.' But Elisha said, 'As the LORD lives, and as your soul lives, I will not leave you!' So they went down to Bethel.

2 Kings 2:1–2

Elijah was one of the most amazing and unique characters of the Old Testament. He was a no-nonsense prophet who shook the nation of Israel by shutting down the heavens for three and a half years and bringing fire from heaven. The land had been polluted by the worship of Baal and corrupted by the wicked reign of King Ahab and his wife, Jezebel. Elijah's ministry brought him into direct confrontation with the powers of darkness after he challenged four hundred and fifty prophets of Baal to a spiritual contest on Mount Carmel. The contest ended with God sending down fire from heaven and the false prophets being killed. Elijah effectively shut down the worship of Baal in Israel at the time.

The time came for Elijah's ministry on earth to end. God had already instructed Elijah to choose Elisha as his successor. Elijah then took his protégé to a city called Gilgal and instructed him to stay there while he (Elijah) proceeded to Bethel. Elisha refused to stay in Gilgal, insisting that he had to accompany Elijah to Bethel. Why did Elisha refuse to stay in Gilgal? Why did Elijah want to proceed to Bethel alone? We cannot authoritatively answer these questions, yet we can apply sanctified common sense to gain insights or lessons that we can apply in our own lives as we pursue God's destiny for our lives. Let us start by examining the city of Gilgal and its significance in this Elijah-Elisha story.

Rolling Away Reproach

Gilgal is the place where Joshua circumcised the second-generation males who had crossed the river Jordan from the wilderness and those who had been born in the wilderness. The first-generation males had died in the wilderness, except for Joshua and Caleb. God commanded Joshua to circumcise these men at Gilgal. "Gilgal" means "rolling away the reproach." The Scripture records that the Lord said to Joshua, "'This day I have rolled away the reproach of Egypt from you.' Therefore, the name of the place is called Gilgal to this day" (Joshua 5:9). Elijah was in effect, telling Elisha, "Stay here, at the place where shame is rolled away, it's a safe place because you don't have to suffer shame." Elisha's spiritual antennae were up, and he was no doubt sensing there was more that God had in store than just rolling away shame from him. Gilgal is no doubt a good place; imagine a place where you suffer no shame, right? Well, it is a good place to begin, but there is more. Gilgal is just like getting a seventy percent passing grade in school but still missing a one hundred percent grade. Gilgal is having a fantastic start, but it is not the finishing line.

Gilgal Is the Place of Salvation

Gilgal is the place where we received salvation. How? The Scriptures tell us that "whoever believes on Him will not be put to shame" (Romans 10:11). Gilgal represents the place where the reproach of sin is rolled away. Remember, the Bible says that "sin *is* a reproach to *any* people" (Proverbs 14:34). Gilgal is the place of our spiritual circumcision. God made a covenant with Abraham to be circumcised as a sign of the covenant. His name was consequently changed from Abram to Abraham. Gilgal is the place where we also get new spiritual identities, where we are called justified instead of condemned. The Scriptures teach that "he who believes in Him is not condemned; but he who does not believe is condemned already, because he has not believed in the name of the only begotten Son of God" (John 3:18). Gilgal is the place where our condemnation was canceled, and we received justification. The reproach and burden of sin are rolled away at salvation, so we can also say Gilgal is the cross.

Elijah was telling Elisha to stay at the place of salvation, but Elisha knew there was more to fulfilling destiny than camping at the cross. Many Christians came to the cross and received justification but refused to go forward. The cross is definitely the foundation of our life and no doubt the most important place, but God wants us to keep growing and going forward. God wants us to graduate from spiritual milk in infancy and progress to eating meat. Many believers are comfortable with spiritual milk forever and have refused to be weaned off this diet. Apostle Paul was in anguish when he addressed the believers at Corinth, for certainly they had come to Gilgal and just camped there. They had refused to grow to maturity.

> *And I, brethren, could not speak to you as to spiritual people but as to carnal, as to babes in Christ. I fed you with milk and not with solid food; for until now you were not able to receive it, and even now you are still not able.*
>
> **1 Corinthians 3:1–2**

The Corinthians had refused to go forward. They were still in Gilgal and were comfortable there. They were content to be saved and have a home in heaven but were unwilling to live purposefully here on earth. Paul is agitated by these believers in Corinth who want to remain in their comfort zone. Gilgal is the place where spiritual milk is plentiful, but there is no spiritual meat. Gilgal is the place where you do not graduate to the next class. The most distinguishing difference between babies and adults is that babies cannot reproduce while adults do. Gilgal is a place of no reproduction because it is not a place of maturity. God's desire is that His children will grow in the faith and, as they mature, bring other sons and daughters into His kingdom. We can discern that Elijah was really testing Elisha's commitment to grow and mature in his walk with God. Elijah was subtly teaching his protégé to learn to go forward. He was telling Elisha that there are other spiritual realms and dimensions he could experience after salvation. What could have become of Elisha if he had just remained in Gilgal? What could he have missed?

Are We Camping in Gilgal?

I have read statistics that indicate the average Christian in America will live and die without winning a single soul to Christ. Imagine a whole life without leading a single soul to the foot of the cross. That is staying in Gilgal and never venturing out. There is so much to experience in God outside the walls of Gilgal. Kindergarten was so much fun for my kids. They taught me many songs they had learned and regaled me with silly little stories that I really enjoyed. They learned a lot, yet a time came for them to progress to first grade and later to middle school and high school. I would be a sad dad indeed if they just wanted to remain in kindergarten just to enjoy the afternoon nap times and songs. We must have the wisdom of Elisha. He could have camped in Gilgal and opened an office there. Why did he have to follow Elijah through several cities? Elijah was about to be taken up into heaven, and Elisha was just about to become the resident prophet, the new spiritual sensation in town.

Do not build a house where you were meant to erect a tent.

The children of Israel were led by a cloud in the day and a pillar of fire at night as they journeyed through the wilderness. They had to move whenever the cloud or the pillar of fire moved.

God has designed our life so that we are able to move forward. It is very unwise to insist on remaining in the place which you should have left. Have you ever tried to fit into a pair of shoes you liked but is now too small for you? The shoes would hurt your toes, and you would walk funny. Many believers are "walking funny" spiritually because they insist on remaining in Gilgal when they should have departed from there a long time ago. I remember being in school with kids that started school quite late, and they were so big they looked like parents. We were all uncomfortable. Determine that you will not camp in Gilgal. Determine you will grow as a believer and progress to Bethel. Spiritual growth is not an accident; it is intentional and hard but worthwhile. *Go forward!*

Go Beyond Bethel

From Gilgal, the two prophets proceeded to the city of Bethel, and once again Elijah said, "Elisha, stay here, please, for the LORD has sent me on to Jericho" (2 Kings 2:4). Elisha had passed the first test. He had refused to be dissuaded from staying in Gilgal and accompanied Elijah all the way to Bethel. "Bethel" literally means "the house of God." This city was previously named Luz but was given the name Bethel by Jacob, Abraham's grandson, while en route to Syria after he had defrauded his brother Esau. Jacob had a great spiritual encounter in the city of Luz where in a dream, he saw the angels of God ascending and descending from a ladder that reached heaven.

> *Then Jacob rose early in the morning, and took the stone that he had put at his head, set it up as a pillar, and poured oil on top of it. And he called the name of that place Bethel; but the name of that city had been Luz previously.*
>
> **Genesis 28:18–19**

Elijah was requesting Elisha to stay in Bethel and not proceed with him to Jericho. Remember, Gilgal is the place of salvation, while Bethel is the house of God, which is the church. Elijah was, in effect, telling Elisha, "Sir, you can now stay here in the house of God, the church. You have already moved a step further from Gilgal, which is salvation, and now you are a member of the church or denomination, which is Bethel." Elisha must have been very spiritually sensitive. He was not yet content. He was determined to go beyond Gilgal and Bethel. Why was he not content with staying in Bethel? What is wrong with just joining a church after we are saved and remaining there all our life?

The Bethel Crowd

Bethel represents the church or the house of God, and many believers are content to camp there. They are happy to move from Gilgal to Bethel, and once their names are written in the church register, they are happy campers. They are completely contented, and if they can get a parking spot not so far from the door and get to sit in the same pew every week, they are ready to wait for the second coming. The Bethel crowd wants to just come to church, meet and fellowship with the Jones and Smith families and go out for Sunday brunch after church. Bethel is a good place to hang out, especially if the preacher is not too demanding, and he better keeps time. The Bethel crowd comes to the church to be served, not to serve. They will put something on the offering plate as it is passed by but are not too radical to tithe every month.

> **The Bethel crowd is in the army of the Lord but always in the reserve. No active duty or going to the front.**

The preacher risks being fired if his sermons are too long. Who wants to get to the fast-food drive-through churches behind all the other Christians from the area?

The Bethel crowd represents the nominal Christian who is in love with the church more than he is in love with Christ. The Bethel crowd is a perfect caricature of the mere façade of religion. God has called us into a relationship, not a religion. Elisha was subtly telling his Master Elijah that belonging to a church is not enough. Relationship and intimacy with Christ are more important than just becoming a member of a church. The church is particularly important, obviously, yet joining a church is not an end in itself; it is a means to an end. Elisha wanted to go forward. Gilgal and Bethel were great blessings but not final destinations. When I drive from Dallas to Houston or Oklahoma City, I will occasionally get into a rest area to stretch my legs or take a bathroom break. I appreciate the blessing and convenience of the facility to travelers, yet the rest area itself is not the purpose or destination of the journey. Do not camp in Bethel; there is more to your life in God! Notice a remarkably interesting episode that happened while Elijah and Elisha were in Bethel. "Now the sons of the prophets who *were* at Bethel came out to Elisha, and said to him, 'Do you know that the LORD will take away your master from over you today?' And he said, 'Yes, I know; keep silent!'" (2 Kings 2:3).

Sons of the Prophets

The sons of the prophets were students being instructed on the ministry of being a prophet, simply prophets-in-training. They knew what was about to happen, but you could almost sense a degree of lethargy and spiritual complacency in them. They come to Elisha to tell him what he already knew, but they do not come to Elijah to ask for any blessing or impartation. I mean, Elijah was the prophet who shut the heavens for three years and prayed fire from heaven. This great prophet is exiting the scene, and the sons of the prophets just stand on the sidelines. They had knowledge but no passion. Elisha shoved them aside and told them to "be silent," modern translation, "just shut up and get out of here!"

The danger of camping at Bethel as a final destination is clothing yourself with the garment of religion. Camping at Bethel comes with the risk of becoming religious at the expense of becoming spiritual. I believe every Christian should be part of a local church, and the Scriptures teach that, but there is way much more than just joining a church after salvation. Elisha did not join the sons of the prophets on the sidelines but proceeded with Elijah to Jericho. In the next chapter, we shall see what Jericho and Jordan represent and how it relates to our journey going forward. Hang tight!

Go Forward Testimony

This is a true story of a woman that I will call Susan to conceal her identity. I met her when I was doing my social work attachment with World Vision Kenya. The lady had a young daughter who was under the sponsorship of World Vision Kenya, and that is how our paths crossed. Her story is long, but I will try to tell it in very few words. Susan was in her twenties, but the sheer horror of her life was mind-boggling. Her life had been a series of tragedies, and she looked a decade older than her actual age.

Susan dropped out of school when she was a sophomore (second year of school) after she became pregnant. The man responsible asked her to move in with her, and a few weeks later, he kicked her out. Susan moved in with her parents and two sisters in a tiny one-room in the slums. The tiny room's walls were made of dirt. The father, though terminally sick, was physically and emotionally abusive to her. The mother then died unexpectedly after a brief illness. She told me that when her mother died, her hopes were also buried. Susan then gave birth to a beautiful baby girl, and shortly thereafter, her former boyfriend and father to her daughter came calling. He seemed remorseful and convinced her to move back with him.

Soon, the man began to seriously assault her, and when she went back to his father, he chased her away, advising her to go back and reconcile with the abusive boyfriend. A relative then advised her to consult a witch doctor, and so they visited one about a hundred miles away. She described a very macabre and dark ritual that was performed on her, which I cannot narrate here. Hell broke loose after the witch doctor's visit. Both of her sisters died in quick succession, and she was pregnant again. The boyfriend then kicked her out again, accusing her of being immoral, and soon he was jailed for theft. She began to have terrible nightmares, with strange beings from nowhere appearing at her bedside in the night and raping her. She began to strip naked and walk in the streets and was arrested and put in a mental asylum. One day, she escaped and came to the streets, and it was at that point that World Vision Kenya heard of her plight and sponsored her daughter.

This is the lady I encountered. I sat and listened to her story, which was many times longer than what I have summarized here. I spent time explaining to her John 8:32 and 2 Corinthians 10:4–5. I then explained the way of salvation to her and ultimately led her to faith in the Lord Jesus Christ. I spent some time teaching her how to pray. I gave her Scriptures to memorize and pray, and I told her I couldn't attend to her unless she did her daily homework, reading and memorizing some verses. I then gave her a strong *prayer prescription.* I gave her verses to proclaim loudly every morning, afternoon, and evening without fail. She became diligent in taking the prayer prescription I had prescribed. I left the attachment program three months later, and the change in Susan was so remarkable. She had joined a local church and was growing in the Lord, and even her pastor had remarked how changed she had become. She was no longer having nightmares and was walking in authority. Wow, what a faithful God we serve!

CHAPTER NINE

BEYOND SPIRITUAL VICTORY

"Then Elijah said to him, 'Elisha, stay here, please, for the LORD has sent me on to Jericho.' But he said, '*As* the LORD lives, and *as* your soul lives, I will not leave you!' So they came to Jericho" (2 Kings 2:4).

Jericho is a picture of spiritual victory. Jericho was the first major city that the children of Israel conquered after they came out of the wilderness under the leadership of Joshua. The Lord had given Joshua a unique battle formula. The children of Israel were to march around the city once for six days and seven times on the seventh day. The city of Jericho was conquered after the walls fell down following the blowing of trumpets by the priests and the people's shouts.

So the people shouted when the priests blew the trumpets. And it happened when the people heard the sound of the trumpet, and the people shouted with a great shout, that the wall fell down flat. Then they went up into the city, every man straight before him, and they took the city.

Joshua 6:20

Elisha was hungry for spiritual victory. He knew that there was no victory without battle and was ready to bear the scars to wear the crown. He was not content to remain in the church, as many believers have. He was willing to step out of the security and comfort of the crowd into the field of battle. Many believers are afraid to step into spiritual warfare, believing this is a sphere of a select few. Spiritual warfare is inevitable, and you are already enrolled whether you know it or not. The children of Israel conquered Jericho by obeying instructions given by God. The basis of defeating our foe is listening to the Lord and following His instructions. We must learn that it is "'not by might nor by power, but by My Spirit,' says the LORD of hosts" (Zechariah 4:6).

The Concept of Battle

The concept of battle sounds very unchristian to the average Christian. Many visualize the Christian life as a perpetually peaceful journey devoid of the scary aspects of warfare. They cannot reconcile God's kingdom of peace with the violence of warfare. They cannot reconcile the God of peace sending His peaceful children into the violence and chaos of warfare.

Many believers that may have a limited understanding of warfare are quick to point out that the battle belongs to the Lord, effectively removing their involvement from any likely cosmic conflict. They see warfare exclusively as a clash between angels and demons, their role being to shout Hallelujah when the battles are won.

Let us examine a few scriptures that will put this concept of spiritual warfare in the right perspective.

First, we are called into warfare.

"For we do not wrestle against flesh and blood, but against principalities, against powers, against the rulers of the darkness of this age, against spiritual *hosts* of wickedness in the heavenly *places*" (Ephesians 6:12). We wrestle, that is the bottom line. Our wrestling, however, is not with men but with dark forces of evil. Second Corinthians 10:3 emphasizes this point by reminding us that "though we walk in the flesh, we do not war according to the flesh."

Secondly, we have weapons that we use in spiritual warfare. The Scriptures describe these weapons thus,

> *For the weapons of our warfare are not carnal but mighty in God for pulling down strongholds, casting down arguments and*

*every high thing that exalts itself against the
knowledge of God, bringing every thought
into captivity to the obedience of Christ.*

2 Corinthians 10:4–5

Thirdly, these weapons that are mighty are also specific, and we are supposed to use them every time. "Put on the whole armor of God, that you may be able to stand against the wiles of the devil" (Ephesians 6:11). The weapons are listed as follows in Ephesians 6:14–18:

A) Belt of Truth

B) Breastplate of Righteousness

C) Gospel of Peace

D) Shield of Faith

E) Helmet of Salvation

F) Sword of the Spirit

G) Prayers and Supplications

Fourthly, we are to be vigilant and alert at all times. The Scriptures remind all and sundry, "no one engaged in warfare entangles himself with the affairs of *this* life, that he may please him who enlisted him as a soldier" (2 Timothy 2:3). We are also reminded by Apostle Peter to "be sober, be vigilant; because your adversary the devil walks about like a roaring lion, seeking whom he may devour" (1 Peter 5:8).

We have a promise from God that we can fight the good warfare and actually win. In fact, we can make the devil run away in morbid fear. James tells us how: "Therefore submit to God. Resist the devil and he will flee from you" (James 4:7).

The above verses give us some insights about spiritual warfare, and I hope at least convinces anyone doubting that we have been called into warfare. The Christian life is not some spiritual buffet where we pick and choose what we fancy and leave out the rest. Elisha was saying to Elijah that he was ready for warfare. He knew warfare may be uncomfortable and tough, yet it is necessary and unavoidable. The day you said yes to Jesus, the forces of darkness automatically unleashed diabolical plans to derail, discourage and destroy you while the forces of heaven aligned to protect and promote you.

Jericho is the place where your enemy meets your God. Jericho is the place the enemy's walls fall down as you sound the trumpet of victory. The walls of Jericho did not fall until the children of Israel were on site and circled that city for seven days. You have to come to the battleground. You cannot send someone else to fight on your behalf. You have to come and fight your battles. The good news is that our victory is not in doubt since greater is He that is in us than he who is in the world.

Crossing the Jordan

Elisha had passed all the tests so far. He was a man intent on spiritual progression. He had refused to just be content with salvation at Gilgal. He had refused to be part of the Bethel crowd and desired more than church affiliation. He had the revelation of the importance of spiritual warfare at Jericho but still desired more. Finally, Elijah heads to the Jordan, the final destination, before being taken up.

"Then Elijah said to him, 'Elisha, stay here, please, for the LORD has sent me on to the Jordan.' But he said, '*As* the LORD lives, and *as* your soul lives, I will not leave you!' So the two of them went on" (2 Kings 2:6). The two prophets walked together, and when they came to the Jordan, something spectacular happened. The Bible records, "Now Elijah took his mantle, rolled *it* up, and struck the water; and it was divided this way and that, so that the two of them crossed over on dry ground" (2 Kings 2:8).

Jordan is the place of the miraculous. Jordan is the place of open heavens, the place of demonstration. Elisha was getting a revelation that the demonstration of God's power was only for those who have been to Gilgal, that is, salvation, then are connected to the body of Christ, that is, Bethel, and have learned to wrestle in battle against forces of darkness, that is Jericho. A cynical and skeptical world steeped in unbelief needs the Gospel not only proclaimed but also demonstrated as well.

Proclamation and Demonstration

Apostle Paul left us nuggets of truth when he addressed the Christians at Corinth, "And my speech and preaching *were* not with persuasive words of human wisdom, but in demonstration of the Spirit and of power" (1 Corinthians 2:4). The apostles in the Book of Acts were used by God to boldly proclaim the Gospel, with signs and wonders accompanying their preaching. "Then fear came upon every soul, and many wonders and signs were done through the apostles" (Acts 2:43). Jesus promised that those who believed would see signs following their preaching. Authentic preaching involves these two parts, proclamation and demonstration. These are like the two wings of an airplane.

We know from reading 2 Kings 2:9 that Elisha eventually asked for a double portion of Elijah's portion, and he got it. Elisha went on to demonstrate God's power in very spectacular ways in his ministry. He had passed the test. He was not content to just receive one level of blessing and settle. The problem with many Christians is that they ask for a double portion in Gilgal, unaware that the double portion is given across the Jordan. Many believers want to camp at Bethel, never venturing outside the comfort and convenience of Bethel, and wonder why they are unsuccessful in spiritual warfare. How will they be warriors when they refuse to proceed to Jericho? The point is Elisha moved forward. He did not let one victory become his last. He celebrated each victory, and when the party was over, he put his trophies in his bag and moved on. Many people do not know when the party is over and squander their lives away, singing of the good old days.

Are you stuck in Gilgal, Bethel, or even Jericho? A great spiritual breakthrough waits for you across the Jordan. It was risky for Elisha to cross the Jordan River when it parted, courtesy of Elijah's mantle with no guarantee it would part again for him alone on his way back, but such is the enterprise of faith.

God wants me and you to go forward. Let us not be like the children of Israel in the wilderness who were told, "You have dwelt long enough at this mountain. Turn and take your journey" (Deuteronomy 1:6b–7). Have you been camping on the mountain of shame, defeat, or discouragement so long you have lost hope of freedom? Rise up, dear friend, square your shoulders, wipe your brow, and look unto Jesus, the Author and Finisher of your faith, and go forward!

Go Forward Testimony

So far, I have narrated go-forward testimonies from Kenya, especially in my younger years in the faith. Let me tell you about a few testimonies from America. God is not limited, and He is at work everywhere. I was studying for my master's degree at Mid-America Baptist Theological Seminary in Memphis, Tennessee. I was in our apartment, at the student housing, watching Pat Robertson on the 700 Club. I was prompted to give to his ministry and called his station to give a small amount, to be deducted every month at a specific date. I had not planned to become a regular giver, but as I sat in my living room that afternoon, I felt a strong urge, and I believe God was asking me to become a regular giver to the ministry. I have given faithfully to the ministry every month without fail for over ten years. The following day, I was called to the office in seminary and informed that a generous giver had walked into the school and paid for the remainder of my school balance. I believe I had one year to go, and my school tuition was paid by someone. To date, I have no idea who it was!

CHAPTER TEN

HE WENT A LITTLE FURTHER

Then Jesus came with them to a place called Gethsemane, and said to the disciples, 'Sit here while I go and pray over there.' And He took with Him Peter and the two sons of Zebedee, and He began to be sorrowful and deeply distressed. Then He said to them, 'My soul is exceedingly sorrowful, even to death. Stay here and watch with Me.' He went a little further and fell on His face, and prayed, saying, 'O My Father, if it is possible, let this cup pass from Me; nevertheless, not as I will, but as You will.'

Matthew 26:36–39 (emphasis mine)

This was Jesus' last day before He was crucified. He knew God's redemption timetable required Him to die on a cruel Roman cross in a matter of hours. Judas Iscariot was on the way with an arresting troop. The remaining eleven disciples were in the garden of Gethsemane with their Master. Jesus then left eight of the disciples in one place and went a little further with Peter, James, and John. Jesus then instructed the three disciples to pray while He went even further and prayed. A powerful lesson can be gleaned from this episode, which will help you in your journey going forward.

The lesson, very simply put, is this: Leaders must go further than their followers. There are three full lists of the twelve apostles of the Lord, namely Matthew 10, Mark 3, and Luke 6. In these three lists, Peter is named first, while Judas Iscariot is named last. In fact, the two sets of brothers, Peter/Andrew and John/James, come on top of every list. Jesus leaves eight of the disciples and gives them a very simple instruction, and that is, "Sit here." Jesus did not ask them to watch and pray. He did not ask them to fast. He did not ask them to be sorrowful. He just asked them to sit there and be still. I know this may sound so simple and basic, but if you have young kids, you know just how hard it is for them to remain still. Maybe the eight were restless and fearful. Jesus knew their level of faith and knew what they could and could not handle. He just asked them to sit and be still. Jesus was a Master Teacher and knew each of His disciples well. He did not have a one-fits-all kind of approach to His disciples.

Jesus then took the three apostles, namely Peter, James, and John, a little further. To whom much is given, much is required. Jesus knew He was preparing these three to give leadership to the church after His death, resurrection, and ascension; therefore, He took them *a little further*. He did not just leave them at the same spot with the eight, but they walked a bit further. Notice that Jesus not only took them further but also gave them a different instruction from the eight. Jesus had asked the eight to simply sit, but when it was the three, probably out of earshot of the eight, He told them, "Stay here and watch with me."

A call to leadership is a call to "walk further." Leadership is about being stretched a little more than those you are leading.

Jesus then left the three and went even further and prayed. I want you to see that picture in your mind. Judas was not anywhere in Gethsemane. He was busy planning the arrest of Jesus. He was untrustworthy and would not go forward in life or ministry. He would be dead in less than three days. The eight were following Jesus, but their faith still needed to be strengthened, so Jesus just told them to sit, probably chit-chat. The three were a bit stronger in the faith, so they were asked to watch. Jesus expected them to pray (but they slept), and finally, Jesus went further than them and prayed.

Prayer and Going Forward

This simple story is pregnant with lessons on going

forward. The first lesson is prayer. Jesus went the furthest and prayed the most. There is a very direct correlation between our commitment to prayer and how far we can go in life. Prayer is often the first casualty of our increasingly busy lives. Jesus was tired, both physically and emotionally, yet He was willing to go further, both physically and spiritually, than His disciples. The three disciples let Him down and were caught sleeping three times. Jesus was about to experience a harrowing time at the hands of His accusers, but His heart was weighed down by more than that. Jesus looked down the lens of time and saw us wallowing in our sins, sickness, bondage, shame, failure, and condemnation. He saw me and you bearing a weight we could not carry and a debt we could not pay. He saw me and you gasping for breath and beckoning for help, struggling under Satan's chokehold. He was weighed down by our condition. Jesus was conviction-driven, not convenience-driven, and that is why He went a little further.

I read a funny line in college that went like this, "Every time I feel like reading, I lie down until the feeling goes." I must admit I was tempted to adopt that as my official school motto, but luckily, I did not. There are many Christians who, when prompted to pray, simply rest until the feeling goes. We must be willing to go a little further, pray a little more and study the Word of God a little more. We must be willing to go further than the average Christian, especially if we want to be entrusted with more responsibility. We find Jesus going to places with the three that He did not go with the rest. Jesus' transfiguration on the mountain happened in the presence of the three and not the others. (See Matthew 17.) Similarly, when Jesus went to Jairus' home to raise his daughter from the dead, He permitted only the parents of the girl and the three apostles. (See Luke 8:51.) The three apostles became the pillars of the Jerusalem church after the ascension of Jesus Christ. The mentoring of Jesus had borne fruit!

He Set His Face

How did Jesus manage to "go forward and further" than His disciples despite the weight that was on His shoulders? There are obviously so many reasons why, but I want to point out only one. Jesus set His face!

"Now it came to pass, when the time had come for Him to be received up, that He steadfastly set His face to go to Jerusalem" (Luke 9:51).

The phrase "set His face" does not just mean He looked towards Jerusalem but rather a firm, unshakable and unbreakable resolve to accomplish His destiny and face a cruel death in Jerusalem. Jesus knew the painful path of redemption would meander through valleys and hills of betrayal, mockery, desertion, beatings, false witnesses, rejection, hunger, thirst, and eventually, a painful cruel death. Jesus knew all this, and yet He "set His face" to go through all this. The question is, why? The answer is that "the joy that was set before Him endured the cross, despising the shame, and has sat down at the right hand of the throne of God" (Hebrews 12:2b).

Jesus looked past the suffering to the glory that would come afterward. He saw the liberty, blessing, and joy that would be ours if He went through this painful redemption plan. He saw the fruit of this endeavor would be richer than the cost of labor.

Paul, the Apostle, was to face a similar predicament years later. A prophet warned him of the danger that lay ahead in Jerusalem, and Luke tells us what happened.

> *And as we stayed many days, a certain prophet named Agabus came down from Judea. When he came down to us, he took Paul's belt, bound his own hands and feet, and said, 'Thus says the Holy Spirit, 'So shall the Jews at Jerusalem bind the man who owns this belt, and deliver him into the hands of the Gentiles." Now when we heard these things, both we and those from that place pleaded with him not to go up to Jerusalem. Then Paul answered, 'What do you mean by weeping and breaking my heart? For I am ready not only to be bound, but also to die at Jerusalem for the name of the Lord Jesus.' So when he would not be persuaded, we ceased,*

saying, 'The will of the Lord be done.'

Acts 21:10–14

Paul was ready and willing to go forward, having embraced his destiny, no matter what lay ahead. The race of faith might sometimes take us through routes and paths we might otherwise wish to avoid. *Going forward* is not a promise of a future devoid of any pain or hiccups. *Going forward* might mean more opposition, difficulties, and all manner of roadblocks mounted on your way, designed either to stop you or slow you down.

The Scripture does not promise or even imply that you are guaranteed a trouble-free or pain-free ride to your destiny. What the Scriptures explicitly teach is that Jesus will never leave nor forsake you.

Jesus told Apostle Peter,

> *'Most assuredly, I say to you, when you were younger, you girded yourself and walked where you wished; but when you are old, you will stretch out your hands, and another will gird you and carry you where you do not wish.' This He spoke, signifying by what death he would glorify God. And when He had spoken this, He said to him, 'Follow Me.'*

John 21:18–19

Jesus tells Peter that he will die a difficult death because of his faith in Christ, and in the same breath, He instructs Peter to keep following Him. He does not give Peter a *get-out-before-it's-too-late* card. He urges Peter to *go forward*, even to certain death, because destiny is that important!

Jesus ran the race that was set before Him. Paul and Peter ran their races. Hundreds of millions of believers have their races and are cheering us from the balconies of glory. Hundreds of millions of believers all over the world are running their races, some under unimaginable challenges and even persecution. *Going forward* is about drawing a line in the sand and choosing the path God ordained for you, whatever terrain you must go through. I am encouraging you today to think of the many thousands who are cheering you on as the writer of Hebrews reminds us,

> *Therefore we also, since we are surrounded by so great a cloud of witnesses, let us lay aside every weight, and the sin which so easily ensnares us, and let us run with endurance the race that is set before us.*

Hebrews 12:1

We have no retreat or surrender options, and in case you are tempted to quit, let these somber words from the mouth of Jesus sober you, "No one, having put his hand to the plow, and looking back, is fit for the kingdom of God" (Luke 9:62).

Go forward in Jesus' name!

Go Forward Testimony

When we relocated from Tennessee to Texas, we stayed in a small apartment for about nine years. The apartment was just slightly under a thousand square feet, and though we have a ton of precious memories of the place, we desired a home of our own. We decided to prepare ourselves, even as we prayed about the issue. I formulated a prayer plan, and for forty days, we prayed together as a family for our dream home. I had earlier asked everyone, that is, my wife and two kids, to get a piece of paper and write what they wanted in the home God would give us. We listed everything, from the number of rooms to the location and so forth. I met our realtor, and when I described the house I wanted and where I wanted it, and then she looked at our income, she began to gently advise where we should consider buying and where our budget indicated. I wanted a place in the suburbs, a generally rich neighborhood with excellent schools and infrastructure. Generally, many people visit so many homes before they settle on one. Our experience was easy and fast.

We put in a bid for a spacious two-story home, slightly over three thousand square feet family home. We won the bid, closed the deal first, and against many odds, we own the home in a great neighborhood. We got what we asked for in a home, only that my daughter had written down on her paper a five-bedroomed home, but all my wife, son, and I had slightly less faith and had written down four bedrooms. My wife had also wanted slightly more bathrooms than what the rest had written down in the paper, and our weak faith in this regard made us compromise on what we got. All in all, we got everything we had agreed on, and in a few months, we have been in our home for five years. God answers prayers!

CHAPTER ELEVEN

FROM CONMAN TO PRINCE

Then Jacob was left alone; and a Man wrestled with him until the breaking of day. Now when He saw that He did not prevail against him, He touched the socket of his hip; and the socket of Jacob's hip was out of joint as He wrestled with him. And He said, 'Let Me go, for the day breaks.' But he said, 'I will not let You go unless You bless me!' So He said to him, 'What is your name?' He said, 'Jacob.' And He said, 'Your name shall no longer be called Jacob, but Israel; for you have struggled with God and with men, and have prevailed.'

Genesis 32:24–28

The name "Jacob" means "conman or supplanter," which is not very flattering. Jacob was quite a character, born holding the heel of his twin brother, Esau. Jacob was a schemer, managing to swindle his brother first, the birthright, and finally, their father's final blessing. You can read the fascinating accounts in the Book of Genesis 25:24–34 and Genesis 27:1–40. Jacob was determined to get what he wanted, even ready to use unorthodox means. He manipulated his hungry brother and negotiated to get Esau's brother a bowl of soup. Esau was obviously a poor businessman, but Jacob was not a fair trader either. A bowl of lentils for a birthright, really? The firstborn son had the birthright, meaning upon the father's death, he was entitled to a double share of the inheritance and automatically became the family head and spokesman in the place of the departed father. Jacob negotiated for all that, and in exchange, he was willing to give his brother only one plate of food! Wow! What was wrong with Esau? I mean, what kind of deal was this?

Esau was not destiny-conscious, while his brother was destiny-hungry.

Family Feud

Jacob, not satisfied with the super deal he had negotiated with his twin brother, had an even greater deal in his mind this time, around with the help of none other than his own mother. Talk of a family feud! Isaac, the father of these twin boys, was quite old, and his eyesight was failing. He requested his son, Esau, to go hunt some game, prepare some award-winning barbecue for him, and come earn his blessing. Esau had lost his birthright through food, and now he had a chance to earn his blessing through food, but guess what? His brother beat him to it. The account is a hair-splitting, on-your-seat-edge true movie of Jacob approaching his medically blind dad with goat meat, not requested wild game. Can you visualize Jacob in your mind's eye, standing before the old man? First, the menu is fake. The old man requested deer meat, and Jacob was standing there with goat meat. Second, he is trying to speak in his brother's voice, although even the dad doubts the voice. Third, because his brother was hairy and he was smooth-skinned, he is wearing the skin of a goat on his neck and arms. (Man, how hairy was Esau??)

Jacob's mother is probably standing a few feet, maybe praying for this scheme to succeed. The con game is successful; apparently, Isaac was losing tastebuds as well and could not tell the difference between deer meat and goat meat. The old saint is full and happy and blesses Jacob with Esau's firstborn blessing. Scarcely had the conniving pair of son and mother left the presence of Isaac when Esau arrived with sizzling deer meat, the stuff he had fed his dad for years. Too late! The dad has a toothpick in his mouth, too full to eat, and yes, the blessing is gone too. Esau then hatched a plan to kill his brother before he could defraud him further, but his brother fled to the home of his uncle Laban in Syria. Jacob met his match in Laban, who spectacularly deceived Jacob. Jacob toiled awfully hard, a full seven years, for Rachel, Laban's daughter, as a wife. He was, however, given a different girl, less beautiful and cross-eyed. He had to labor another seven years to get Rachel. He worked another six years, taking care of livestock, a total of twenty years. Payback time!

Jacob finally had enough of Laban's shenanigans and decided to flee. He then encountered a heavenly visitor who wrestled with him the entire night. Jacob was unwilling to let go of his wrestling partner, insisting on getting a blessing before the fight was over. The visitor from heaven then changed his name, in essence, his identity, when he told him to drop the name Jacob and answer to the name "Israel," which means "prince." Imagine that, from conman to prince.

A conman has to scheme, lie, steal, and manipulate to obtain. A prince obtains by inheritance and by virtue of being the son of the king.

A prince rides on the favor and power of the king and already has access to all that is within the king's dominion. Jacob did not have to lie to his father, manipulate his brother or connive with his mother. In fact, when he met his brother, Esau, after his name was changed to prince, he gave him a gift of animals, running into a few million dollars in today's currency.

What is our takeaway lesson here? Going forward in life is not a matter of your clever schemes, manipulation, lies, or dishonest gain. Going forward is a matter of surrender to God.

> **Going forward is a matter of being stripped of our human strength and being clothed with God's strength.**

Going forward is a matter of getting a new identity in God, where our human ingenuity is dwarfed by God's grace and favor. We go forward when we have an encounter with God, and our self-will is broken. Jacob had a limp after the wrestling night encounter. A limp is a symbol of physical weakness, but remember the words of Apostle Paul, "When I am weak, then I am strong" (2 Corinthians 12:10b).

Danger of Complacency

Jacob's conniving streak can only be matched by Esau's complacency. Esau had little appetite for weighty matters of destiny. How do you sell your birthright for one plate of food? Proverbs 1:32b says that the "complacency of fools will destroy them." Spiritual appetite is a prerequisite to spiritual progress. You cannot really go forward if you are always indifferent, apathetic, and averse to even slight discomfort. What if Esau refused to sell his birthright for a meal; do you think he would have died of hunger that night? He was not starving, there was no famine, and he was not a prisoner denied food. Apathy will make you pay too much! "Blessed are those who hunger and thirst for righteousness, for they shall be filled" (Matthew 5:6). Esau came from a great heritage of faith. His grandfather was Abraham, the father of faith, while his dad was the son of promise. His other relatives are all listed in the Bible's hall-of-fame in Hebrews 11. Isaac, his father, even gave him a conditional blessing in Genesis 27:40, "By your sword you shall live, and you shall serve your brother; and it shall come to pass, *when you become restless, that you shall break his yoke from your neck*" (emphasis mine). Isaac was, in effect, telling his son that the day he would become tired of playing second fiddle to his brother Jacob, he would break that domination. What else could he do for Esau?

Esau sacrificed the eternal to satisfy the temporal. He carried spiritual truth lightly and esteemed fleshy satisfaction. Jacob was a supplanter, yes, but there is one thing you could not take away from him, and that is spiritual hunger. He was weak but had a desire for God and was hungry to fulfill his destiny. Jacob's hunger for spiritual truth earned him a permanent place as one of the three patriarchs of the Old Testament so that we know to say "the God of Abraham, Isaac, and Jacob." Hunger is a sign of health. The first thing you lose when you get sick is your appetite. Never lose appetite for the things of God. Never lose the desire to go forward and fulfill your

CHAPTER ELEVEN: FROM CONMAN TO PRINCE

destiny. The journey may be tough. The turbulence may be extreme, the storms raging, the winds strong, and the horizon blurred, but you keep going forward. Do not quit now because "our salvation *is* nearer than when we *first* believed" (Romans 13:11b).

Go Forward Testimony

I was very annoyed by the very loud and persistent knocking on my door in the middle of the day, so I did not bother to open the door. I was in the bathroom, shaving in our apartment. Suddenly, someone jumped into my patio, and when I went to check, a guy jumped out and sprinted towards their getaway car. I ran out, fueled by adrenaline, chasing down the thug through the parking lot. The gateway vehicle sped out, and after a short while, I came to my senses and returned back quickly to my apartment. What was I doing chasing a thug who may have been armed with a gun while I was unarmed? My kids were in the house, and God had spared us from any danger. The very loud knocking was an attempt by the thugs to test whether somebody was in the house. They had intended to break in from the window by the patio, which would have let them into the house through the kid's bedrooms.

A similar incident happened many years later in the home we currently live in. My neighbor called me at work, just around the time my daughter got home from high school. They had just come face to face with a man who emerged from our backyard, scaling a high wall. The neighbor asked him what he was doing in our backyard, and the startled young man ran away. We have no idea how he got back there nor what his intentions were, only that he did not get into our house or steal anything from the yard. He ran away before the neighbor could get her husband, who was working inside their home. The young man escaped, and just then, my daughter arrived home from school. No one else was home at the time. God protected us again. Two similar incidents, two similar outcomes. We constantly plead for the protection of our lives and property in our family prayers. Psalm 91 is a particularly favorite scripture of protection that we invoke in our homes.

CHAPTER TWELVE

THE DAY I CALLED THE PRESIDENT'S OFFICE

Ignorance can sometimes be bliss. The story I am about to tell you is embarrassing to me now, not then. I finished university at the age of twenty-four. My first job had a big title, but the pay was meager. I worked for a small company called Coalex Africa Ltd, which would import coal from South Africa and market it to mainly tea factories in Kenya as an alternative and cost-effective fuel instead of wood or oil. The company was still relatively young and was still trying to break ground. My pay as a marketing executive was the equivalent of one hundred and fifty US dollars monthly. I was dating a beautiful girl, today my wife of twenty years, and we were planning our wedding. The wedding date was April 27, 2002. I was thinking about the wedding guest list about six weeks prior to the wedding, and suddenly, a thought crossed my mind (which I know for sure was not from the Lord), *Why not invite the president of Kenya to my wedding?* (Oh, the ignorance and innocence of youth.)

I checked the president's office telephone number from the telephone book, called the yellow pages then, and dialed the number, leaning on my swinging chair. Suddenly, a husky voice answered, "Yes, this is Harambee House; how can I help you?" "Well, my name is Patrick Kariuki, I have a wedding coming up in about two months, and I was calling to invite the president, and I wanted to pass by your office and drop the invitation card, sir." I paused to hear the response. I cannot recall whether the man at the other end sounded amused or astounded, but he gave me a mouthful about protocol and process. He told me the president is a busy man and would not just grace a wedding with a two-month notice. He was not rude but made me aware of how ridiculous I sounded to imagine just walking nonchalantly to the president's office to invite him to my wedding. In case you are wondering, the government of Kenya was not represented at my wedding. I have since matured to understand what protocol is and how it works. Oh, the audacity of youth!

Faith versus Presumption

I had obviously acted out of faith but out of presumption. I had seen on television the president attending weddings of fellow citizens, and so I assumed I just needed to make a call and drop a card of invitation. I thought I was operating on faith, but I was really being presumptuous. How do we know if we are operating on faith or if we are being presumptuous?

The Bible says faith comes by hearing, and hearing by the word of God (Romans 10:17). Faith, therefore, is hearing God and obeying His voice. Faith is not present if God's voice is absent.

Faith is not attempting great feats for God or embarking on big projects. Faith is not doing something you have never done before or undertaking a humongous task. Faith is obeying an instruction from God, big or small. God never told me to invite the president to my wedding, so I was not acting on faith. A story that illustrates this difference between faith and presumption is documented in the Book of Numbers. A little background for context will suffice. Moses is ready to lead the children of Israel into the promised land, and according to Numbers 13, he sent twelve men, among them Joshua and Caleb, to spy on the land. The men go to Canaan and spy on the land for forty days, and upon their return, ten of the men give a discouraging report, in essence saying they should not even dare to go try possessing the land since the inhabitants of the land were giants, much bigger and stronger than them. The entire population of the children of Israel weeps with fear.

God pronounces severe judgment on the entire congregation since they had bitterly complained against Moses and Aaron, the high priest. The males twenty years and above would die in that wilderness because they did not believe God to give them the land and would not go in to possess the land. The people sat and listened to Moses outlining how God would punish them and kill them in the wilderness, and when they heard the scary report, they did something they thought was faith but was just presumption. Here is the summary of the story.

> *Then Moses told these words to all the children of Israel, and the people mourned greatly. And they rose early in the morning and went up to the top of the mountain, saying, 'Here we are, and we will go up to the place which the LORD has promised, for we have sinned!' And Moses said, 'Now why do you transgress the command of the LORD? For this will not succeed. Do not go up, lest you be defeated by your enemies, for the LORD is not among you. For the Amalekites and the Canaanites are there before you, and you shall fall by the sword; because you have turned away from the LORD, the LORD will not be with you.' But they presumed to go up to the mountaintop. Nevertheless, neither the ark of the covenant of the LORD nor Moses departed the camp. Then the Amalekites and the Canaanites who dwelt in that mountain came down and attacked them, and drove*

them back as far as Hormah.
Numbers 14:39–45 (emphasis mine)

God spoke the first time, and they refused to go in, weeping and complaining because of the report they heard from the ten spies. God proclaimed His judgment, and when they heard it, they presumptuously arose to go and possess the land. Moses called their bluff, but they disobeyed and went to fight the Amalekites and the Canaanites. They were chased down the mountain like bees because they were not acting on faith but presumption. Going forward is not just making big grandiose plans and setting out a plan to achieve them. Going forward is not just having a big dream or goal and pursuing it.

Going forward is getting a blueprint of one's life from God and then obeying the heavenly vision. I want you to go forward, but the journey does not really start in your heart: it starts in the mouth of God.

Faith is hearing what God says and then embarking on the journey of obedience. May God speak, so we can go forward!

Go Forward Testimony

My family has many testimonies of God's faithful interventions both in our nuclear family and also in our extended family. We have seen diseases heal, both miraculously without the intervention of medicine and also through treatment in hospitals. We have seen God provide miraculously but also provide through the jobs he has provided to us. My son was recently gifted a car, a Honda Element, by a very close and dear family from Tennessee. The lady has also bought clothes and gifts for our children for more than ten years, several times driving five hundred miles one way to come to visit us and spend time with the kids.

Time and space would fail me to mention the daily protection on the roads from accidents and protection from diseases. Many times, God protects us from dangers that we were not even aware of, and so it is not even possible to enumerate all the testimonies one by one. We would do well to heed this encouragement from King Solomon.

"Trust in the LORD with all your heart, and lean not on your own understanding; in all your ways acknowledge Him, and He shall direct your paths" (Proverbs 3:5–6).

SECTION TWO

HOW TO GO FORWARD

CHAPTER THIRTEEN

ADMIT YOU HAVE A PROBLEM

Have you ever encountered someone who obviously was struggling in an area of their lives, but they were adamant they could fix it? How many people have been hopelessly addicted to alcohol or other substance, and when confronted, they insist, "Well, I can quit any time I want." Many times, human pride causes us, to some degree, to live in denial of the existence of a problem that we would need a stronger hand to solve. We have an I-got-this attitude even when we have no clue how to navigate from whatever situation we could be dealing with. I remember my family and I were driving from Dallas, Texas, to Memphis, Tennessee, one afternoon, and my wife noticed the fuel gauge was almost at empty. My wife, out of an abundance of caution, insisted I pull over at the very next gas station to fuel. My son and daughter joined in the chorus, and all were getting on my nerves, to be honest. I insisted everything was in control, and to prove I was really in charge, I drove past a few gas stations. We were going around a bend on the highway on the outskirts of Memphis when the car was out of fuel and almost stalled in the middle of the highway. God helped me to pull over on the shoulder, and a motorist gave me a ride to the nearest gas station to buy gas. My wife and kids were not happy campers, and the conversation was muted for the rest of the journey.

Basic as it may sound, the first step to really going forward is to admit or acknowledge that you have a problem, admit you need help, or admit something needs to get fixed.

66

You cannot resolve what you cannot admit.

God made us to thrive only as we depend on Him, and Jesus categorically stated, "Without Me you can do nothing" (John 15:5b). Conversely, Apostle Paul stated emphatically, "I can do all things through Christ who strengthens me" (Philippians 4:13). You were made to have a vertical relationship with God and a horizontal relationship with people. You cannot really thrive and be on your optimal performance if either your vertical or horizontal relationship is dislocated.

> **God almost always sends help to you through other people, and often you will have to be vulnerable to both God and some people for you to receive help for whatever it is you need.**

What are a few considerations in admitting we have a problem? We cannot obviously enumerate all of them, but here are a few major roadblocks we must dismantle in order to admit we have a problem.

Deal with Denial

Denial is the typical default position when we are in a terrible fix, whether we are dealing with grief, divorce, job loss, shame, or simply keeping our rooms clean and organized. Admitting we have a problem that our skill level cannot match or solve requires a level of vulnerability, and no one wants to be vulnerable.

> **The I-got-this posture is all too common, and sometimes the price tag for being obstinate is too steep.**

The root cause of this is human pride, and King Solomon reminds us that "a man's pride will bring him low, but the humble in spirit will retain honor" (Proverbs

29:23). A nurse narrated to me once how difficult it was dealing with a doctor who was a patient in the hospital she worked. The sick doctor disregarded medical advice from fellow physicians and was hardly appreciative of the care given by the nurses. I imagine it was difficult for the doctor who used to help his patients to be the one who depended on others to help him overcome his sickness. We may be facing a humiliating prospect, a debilitating loss, a very unpleasant situation, or a frightening issue, yet denial will not take you even one inch closer to the solution. There is a chance that maybe you have encountered a major episode that produced a lot of grief or betrayal in your life. You may have been in denial for a while, unable to reconcile the facts of the situation and what the ideal would have been. Admitting you have a problem or there is a problem is the first step in going forward.

Admitting we have a problem will not automatically resolve it, but it is a vital beginning point toward finding a solution. Admitting we have a problem may seem like a weakness, but it is actually a strength. When we admit that we need a hand that is stronger than ours, we are not being weak but strong. Admitting that we need more than what we have is a good strategy since we make room for help from someone else. The strength of another added to our own does not make us weaker in any way; after all, "two *are* better than one, because they have a good reward for their labor. For if they fall, one will lift up his companion. But woe to him *who is* alone when he falls, for *he has* no one to help him up" (Ecclesiastes 4:9–10).

Deal with Pride

Oh boy, this is a big one, isn't it? How many people have fallen off an emotional, financial, or spiritual cliff because they were too proud to seek help? How many people walk up and down the aisle of Walmart looking for an item for a long time simply because they will not ask for help from a store associate? How many people are too proud to ask for help, even when they clearly need it, simply because they detest the idea of looking weak? Pride is not always obvious and easy to detect, especially when we are dealing with the man in the mirror.

Pride is sometimes very subtle and hidden, buried deep within us and masquerading as personal confidence or strength.

Pride will keep you from asking for help when you should and will keep you from receiving help when it is within reach.

Pride is really not a strength: it is a terrible weakness. It takes strength to reach out for help and takes strength to receive help.

Admitting you have a problem or you need some help will not be possible unless and until you deal with the problem of pride. Pride is actually the original sin since Lucifer (Satan) fell when he sought to be equal to God. Lucifer was created an incredibly beautiful, magnificent, and glorious being, and when pride entered his heart, the downfall was inevitable. The Scriptures remind us of all that "pride *goes* before destruction, and a haughty spirit before a fall" (Proverbs 16:18). The opposite of pride is humility, and it is a powerful and profitable trait to have. Humility is a perpetual staircase that only takes you up. Apostle Peter reminds us that "God resists the proud, but gives grace to the humble" (1 Peter 5:5b). Pride will block you from admitting you need help. Humility will lead you to seek help, or at least help you admit you need help. The Scriptures are full of men and women that were too proud to admit they needed help, leading to their destruction, and stories of others who humbled themselves and sought help, eschewing imminent destruction. The Scriptures admonish us to be "clothed in humility," and in every possible scenario, humility is always an asset while pride is always a liability.

Deal with Fear

Fear is an extraordinarily strong motivation. The Bible, which is both God's love letter to us and an instruction manual for successful living, has much to say on the subject of fear. The bottom line is this, fear not! Fear will keep you from so much that God intended for you. You will not be able to go forward and achieve all you were destined to achieve if fear is your dominant emotion. Tackling or overcoming fear is beyond the scope of this book, but suffice it to say that "God has not given us a spirit of fear, but of power and of love and of a sound mind" (2 Timothy 1:7). They say hindsight is 20/20, and looking back, I can count many blessings I have missed just because I was afraid. People I should have approached, others I should have confronted, projects I should have undertaken, investments I should have taken up, and so forth. I am sure you can find your own list where fear was the main catalyst that kept you from God's best.

You have to be willing to deal with fear. You have to choose that in spite of fear; you will do it if you believe it ought to be done.

You may not always have the option of eliminating all the fear before you take the first step; sometimes, you just start in spite of fear.

Do you want to go forward? You have to admit you have a problem, and this involves dismantling at least three roadblocks, namely denial, pride, and fear!

My Skydiving Experience

I have always had a fear of heights. I remember a summer job while in seminary, where I worked for a home improvement company. We spray-painted buildings, filled cracks in the driveway and cleaned gutters, and did minor roof repairs. I can vividly remember how dizzying it felt to be on the roof. I vowed at one time that if God took me off one particular roof safely, I would not put myself on another roof, and I have not! I cannot explain how I had such a great fear of heights yet secretly nursed a burning desire to skydive. One day my family was visiting a friend, and I met a lady who had just gone through a painful divorce. She narrated how she decided to go skydiving as a way of dealing with her pain. Her reasoning, which was genius, was that skydiving, being the most fearful action she could personally contemplate, would help her conquer her fear of dealing with her new divorced status. She rekindled my desire to do skydiving, and about ten years ago, I conquered that fear and jumped off a plane from ten thousand feet in the air. The experience will stay with me for life. Do it, afraid! (I do not know who said that, but I like it, don't you?)

The Process of Admitting a Problem

The process of admitting you have a problem is three-fold. *First, you must admit it to yourself.* The quote,

"To thine own self be true," is attributed to William Shakespeare in Hamlet. You must be brutal to yourself. You have to look in the mirror and indict the man or woman that is staring back at you. Call the problem by its name. If you are dealing with lust, do not say you have a problem with looking at women. No, you have a problem with lust and deal with it as such. If you steal, do not say you have a problem with other people's things. No, you do not have a problem with people's things. How can you even deal with something you will not even accurately label? Write down the issue or problem accurately and comprehensively. Do not let denial, pride, or fear stop you. This is the beginning of your freedom.

Secondly, you must admit it to God. This is called confessing. Confess to God freely and truthfully. Tell Him exactly what you want or need. God is not intimidated by your feelings, questions, or emotions. Speak with Him loudly in a secluded place, just you and Him. God is the only One who can truly set you free. A program can help to modify your behavior or routine, but there is no program on earth that can truly transform your heart. Speak to God; He is always listening.

Thirdly, you may admit it to a friend. Please notice I used the word *may* as opposed to the word *must* in this instance. You may find it necessary to confess to someone else, a mature, trustworthy person, like a pastor or spouse, for accountability, support, or counsel. Many times, this may be necessary for true healing to occur, yet sometimes it might be an issue just between you and God. "Confess *your* trespasses to one another, and pray for one another, that you may be healed" (James 5:16a).

CHAPTER FOURTEEN

DECIDE YOU WANT HELP

This may sound rather obvious, right? You might be surprised by the sheer number of people who may admit they have a problem but have not yet decided they need help or need it yet. Not everyone who has a problem is looking for a solution. There are many who have a problem that they have learned to tolerate. There are many people who have acquired learned helplessness and have no courage to face whatever problem they are facing. There are many people who are too afraid to face their problems and have decided they can only learn to cope with the problem rather than try to solve it. The presence of a problem does not automatically translate to the seeking of a solution.

The agony of a problem sometimes presents a lighter challenge than the burden of change to some people, and they have built a support mechanism around the problem.

There are many people that have become so attached to the pity, attention, assistance, and sympathy granted to them that they have learned to accommodate, tolerate and even excuse the problem. Beware, especially as a caregiver or if you engage in alleviating human distress, that not everyone who is bleeding is looking to be bandaged or healed. Not everyone who is distressed is truly seeking a resolution.

You cannot truly help anyone who is not fully decided they need help.

Deep Pockets, Shallow Heart

The Book of Mark tells of a young, rich ruler who came to Jesus and asked Him, "Good Teacher, what shall I do that I may inherit eternal life?" (Mark 10:17b). Jesus then went down the list of the Ten Commandments, and to his credit, the young man had observed all of them. Jesus reached to the depth of the young man's heart and asked him to sell all he had and then follow Jesus, "but he was sad at this word, and went away sorrowful, for he had great possessions" (Mark 10:22). The young man had many admirable qualities. He was moral, having kept all the Ten Commandments from his youth. He was rich and a leader in his community. He was no doubt an incredibly good role model to other young men in his community, but he had a problem that Jesus sought to address. He not only had possessions, but the possessions had him as well. Jesus was not trying to dispossess him but was trying to give him true riches. He had a heart problem that Jesus wanted to heal, but the young man walked away sad. He walked away a poor man with a lot of money. He walked away with his heart problem unhealed. The rich young ruler had deep pockets but a shallow heart.

What would have become of that young man if he had heeded Jesus? What if he sold everything and gave all the proceeds to the poor, and followed the Lord? The Lord would have given him true riches, and the desires of his longing heart would have been fulfilled. Moses, by contrast, "when he became of age, refused to be called the son of Pharaoh's daughter, choosing rather to suffer affliction with the people of God than to enjoy the passing pleasures of sin" (Hebrews 11:24–25). Moses was raised in the palace of the most powerful king at the time, enjoying every privilege and trappings of power Egypt could give and yet could not trade all that comfort for his destiny. He refused to be swayed by the pomp and pageantry of the palace and identified with his brothers, who were slaves. Your destiny is much more valuable than wealth, power, or privilege. The young ruler lacked this revelation and could not give up his earthly possessions for a front-row seat to serve humanity with the Creator of the universe.

Do You Want to Be Made Well?

The Book of John narrates the story of a man who had been crippled for thirty-eight years, and like many in his condition, he laid by the pool of Bethesda. He waited there "for an angel went down at a certain time into the pool and stirred up the water; then whoever stepped in first, after the stirring of the water, was made well of whatever disease he had" (John 5:4). Jesus then met that man, who had been trying to get well for that very long time and asked him, "Do you want to be made well?" (John 5:6b). Now, think about it, why would Jesus really ask a man crippled for thirty-eight years if he wanted to be healed. I mean, this man had been camping at the healing pool waiting for the angel that stirred the healing waters, but being crippled, someone got in first before him. How could Jesus ask him such a question? Was Jesus being insensitive or uncaring? Far from it! Jesus was looking deep into the heart of the man. Jesus was doing a spiritual surgery on the man and seeing in the man what no one else had ever seen.

To understand why Jesus asked the man what would appear to be a rhetorical question, we would need to examine the response the man gave to the Lord. He said, "Sir, I have no man to put me into the pool when the water is stirred up; but while I am coming, another steps down before me" (John 5:7). Jesus asked him a direct yes or no answer. Jesus knew the man had been there a long time; He knew the man had no one to put him in the stirred pool and all the other details. Jesus was not looking for an explanation or an excuse. Jesus was not looking for a head answer but a heart answer. The man obviously desired to be healed; otherwise, he would not have camped there that long, but he had somehow learned to cope with his problem. He had come to believe that there was probably no hope or help. He had probably been advised that when life gives you lemons, you make lemonade, and so he had made some lemonade from these bitter lemons and learned to cope. He had probably been advised to lower his expectations and probably was no longer so enthusiastic about the arrival of the angel that usually stirred the healing waters. The man's bigger problem was a heart problem, not a leg problem. His deeper issue was spiritual, not physical. Most of our problems come from within, not from without. Do you really want to go forward? Have you fully decided in your head and persuaded in your heart? I want to give you the two-tier process or stage of fully deciding to go forward.

The Head Connection

The first step in deciding is what I call the head connection or the intellectual assent. We are rational beings equipped with the ability to make choices.

We have free will and the ability to make a choice, and before we really go forward, we must first sit down and make a decision. Listen to these words of Jesus,

> *For which of you, intending to build a tower, does not sit down first and count the cost, whether he has enough to finish it—lest, after he has laid the foundation, and is not able to finish, all who see it begin to mock him, saying, 'This man began to build and was not able to finish'? Or what king, going to make war against another king, does not sit down first and consider whether he is able with ten thousand to meet him who comes against him with twenty thousand? Or else, while the other is still a great way off, he sends a delegation and asks conditions of peace.*
>
> **Luke 14:28–32**

Jesus is teaching more than one lesson here, but an obvious lesson is that before you embark on a major project, you must sit down and decide. There are many considerations and deliberations, but the bottom line is this: a decision has to be reached eventually. You can hear a thousand sermons, you can be prayed over a hundred times, and you can sit under the most inspiring motivational teachers and anointed preachers, but you will never go forward until you personally make the choice to do so.

The Holy Spirit can inspire and quicken you, yet you must still make the choice to cooperate with His help.

"I call heaven and earth as witnesses today against you, *that* I have set before you life and death, blessing and cursing; therefore choose life, that both you and your descendants may live" (Deuteronomy 30:19). Clearly, God is stating here that He has given us the power to choose or pick between options.

Adam was given the ability to make a choice in the Garden of Eden. God forbid him to eat from the tree of knowledge of good and evil, but He did not fence the tree with an electric fence or put it out of Adam's reach. Adam had a choice to obey or disobey, and he chose to disobey. Yes, I know about the snake and Eve, but Adam still chose to eat the forbidden fruit. He was not under duress or ultimatum from his wife. Eve chose to eat the fruit, and she had the power to overrule the serpent. You will never go forward until and unless you decide to. You may have to do more than just decide, but this step is impossible to skip. Many people are stuck, waiting on God to do something about their condition. God has done everything He will ever do; He sent Jesus Christ, who also did everything He will ever do, and Christ, in turn, sent the Holy Spirit. When will you realize that all the help you will ever need has been availed and all you need to kick start the process is making a decision? Decision-making is really the very first step of the journey, and the truth is that it is one thing God cannot do for you.

The Heart Connection

The second stage in making a decision is what we shall call the heart connection, and for lack of a better term, the passion, energy, or the fire to go forward.

The head connection is the beginning point, but the heart connection provides the motivation to start and the momentum to continue. Many times, we know what we ought to do, and actually, we plan to do it, but we run out of steam or motivation to keep going. We abandon plans we have thought out because we run out of zeal. Consider what was written concerning Christ, "Then His disciples remembered that it was written, 'Zeal for Your house has eaten Me up'" (John 2:17). This statement was made after Jesus made a whip of cords and drove all the merchants that were doing business in the temple. They observed Jesus' anger at the audacity of those who had converted the temple into a marketplace. They observed Jesus' energy in overturning the merchants' tables and driving these men out of the temple. They concluded He was consumed by *zeal*. He had a *heart connection* to the work His Father had sent Him to do.

Listen to what Prophet Isaiah had prophesied about Jesus about seven hundred years earlier. Pay close attention to the last line.

> *Of the increase of His government and peace there will be no end, upon the throne of David and over His kingdom, to order it and establish it with judgment and justice from that time forward, even forever. The zeal of the LORD of hosts will perform this.*

Isaiah 9:7

We get a glimpse of what the job description of the Messiah would be, but we are also informed that this will be accomplished through the zeal of the Lord. Do you see the connection? He would be zealous, meaning His heart would be fully immersed in the work, not just the head. Jesus was on the go, diligent and relentless, from the day He was baptized by John the Baptist to the day He was crucified. The apostles were on the go from the day they were endued with power on the day of Pentecost.

We need to have both the head and the heart connections to go forward. We must sit down and count the cost as was alluded to above. We must have a mental understanding of where we want to go and devise a plan on how to get there. We might have to read up on stuff, research, discuss, evaluate, consult, and do whatever we need to have an understanding. We cannot skip this part, but we also have to have the energy, the zeal, and the fire to keep us going through the process. Going forward requires both the head connection and the heart connection.

CHAPTER FIFTEEN
COUNT THE COST

I have good news and bad news; which should I serve you first? Well, let me start with the good news. The good news is that you can go forward, but the bad news is that it is going to cost you. You will simply not make a costless voyage to your desired haven. Freedom is costly, and so is greatness, success, or any other virtue that you admire. Changing your life will cost you more than mere pocket change; it is a pretty pricey affair. Sit down, and let us do the math!

I do not know to whom this is attributed to, but he/she said, "If you think education is expensive, try ignorance." I can say, in the same line of wisdom, "If you think freedom is costly, try bondage." What do I mean? I mean, the decision to change and go forward is still the better option, no matter the price tag it is going to carry. The price tag for not changing is higher, even though it is delayed. Many people mistakenly assume that if they do not do the heavy lifting associated with change, then they will just auto-pilot their life, not achieving their life's best, but they will equally escape the grueling pain of trying to change. The truth is if you live a mediocre life, never stepping outside your comfort zone and never embracing painful sacrifice, it will cost you so much more, even if later in life. The bill collector may not come now, but he will eventually come calling, and most likely when you cannot pay! Imagine neglecting your health, eating junk food, imbibing alcohol now, partying entire weekends, and denying your body rest in your thirties or forties.

Your body may have the strength to absorb all these foolish indulgencies, but somewhere in your fifties or sixties, the price you may have to pay is very steep. The opportunities missed as a youth may mean a steep price to pay in adulthood. Listen to the words of the wisest man that ever lived, "Remember now your Creator in the days of your youth, *before the difficult days come*, and the years draw near when you say, 'I have no pleasure in them'" (Ecclesiastes 12:1, emphasis mine). You cannot neglect your spiritual, mental, physical, and financial health and not pay dearly later in life. Remember the story of the prodigal son who inherited a lot of possessions and went far away from home to enjoy the largesse? What happened after the money bag was empty? He was in want, and nobody gave him anything! The point is both changing and not changing will cost you, and so our focus in this is paying the cost of change. What exactly is the price tag for change? Let us explore three major bills you will have to foot for positive change.

The Cost of Convenience

Positive change will greatly inconvenience you. You will be inconvenienced in growing spiritually, professionally, financially, physically, or mentally. Going forward is not necessarily a comfortable journey, and you must be willing to sacrifice convenience and comfort.

Growth comes with stretching, whichever way you look at it, and stretching is inconvenient.

A mother carrying life in her womb will have to be inconvenienced in order to bring forth the precious baby. She cannot carry life in her and insist on keeping her perfect figure. The mere fact that life has been conceived means that convenience has to be conceded. The mother has to give up a lot of convenience because of the life she is carrying. She has to watch what she eats and drinks, activities she has to engage in or avoid, and so forth. The birth of the baby will obviously bring a lot of changes as the young one is being slowly shaped into a responsible and respectable member of society.

Jesus said, "Most assuredly, I say to you, unless a grain of wheat falls into the ground and dies, it remains alone;

but if it dies, it produces much grain" (John 12:24). The grain of wheat does not have to die, but then it will not multiply. The option is to fall to the ground and die, and only then will life, and multiplied, come forth. The process of falling to the ground and actually dying does not excite our natural sensibilities. This is such a conundrum; how does life come out of death? Why does a seed, which is seeking life, have to die? Isn't life the opposite of death? That is a deep mystery, but that seed must, in a sense, lose its current life (die) in order to gain a new, vibrant, and abundant life; this time around, not just as a single lonely seed, but with many other seeds. Jesus had to die for us to live. His death, as a seed, brought forth many sons to glory, as the Scriptures teach in Hebrews 2:10.

Do you want to go forward? Do you desire to progress in your life? You better get comfortable with the idea of discomfort. You better deem it convenient to be inconvenienced. They say you cannot eat your cake and keep it. You will make sacrifices to grow spiritually, financially, mentally, socially, or psychologically. Look, if you are looking for a solution that will cost you nothing, you will end up with a solution that is not worth holding. King David refused a free offer of land and bulls to offer sacrifices to stop a deadly plague in Israel. Araunah had both offered the land, the oxen, and the wood for free, but David said these important words, "No, but I will surely buy *it* from you for a price; nor will I offer burnt offerings to the LORD my God with that which costs me nothing"

(2 Samuel 24:24). The idea of a costless sacrifice was repugnant to David. One of the great tragedies of our modern worship is yielding to the temptation to do with just the barest minimal, not going the extra mile. The bottom line is: if it costs you nothing, it is probably not worth it.

The Cost of Coaching

I use the term "coaching" in a broad sense to include but not limited to all the necessary training, resources, mentoring and/or any external sources of help you might need. There are times you may need to consult and reach out for help.

There are people who have gone further than you in the direction you wish to go, and they may have personal or professional tips to help you along your journey.

You may have to consult a few books, go to a seminar, get a life coach, enroll in some kind of program, or simply get an accountability partner or sign up for some kind of buddy system. I have put all these together under the broad title of coaching.

You ask, is coaching really mandatory if I have to go forward in life? I will say a big fat yes! The mere fact that you are trying to go further indicates you need some kind of help or encouragement, and you would have been that far much earlier if it were all you had needed was you. I obviously know you will have to do much of the heavy lifting, but you will need some kind of help. The Scriptures state unequivocally that "two *are* better than one, because they have a good reward for their labor" (Ecclesiastes 4:9). Depending on the complexity of your situation or the height you want to reach, you will need different kinds of coaching or mentorship. You may not need to hire some guru or buy some expensive program if all you need is to keep a healthy habit you have started on-going. You might just opt to have a buddy system, an accountability partner to hold you accountable and encourage you. A specific prescription for your specific career goals or in-depth professional help is beyond the immediate scope and goal of this book, but mine is to urge you to look within and without for help to get to your next level.

I must admit I have become open to the idea of having a personal trainer or life coach for some aspects of my life. I have come to appreciate the fact that God, in His infinite wisdom, put some wisdom in other people that could be of great value to my life. Similarly, God has deposited in me some wisdom that could be utilized by someone else. To go forward, I would highly recommend you consider the type and intensity of coaching that you need in your life. I believe you will go further in life if you allow others to invest in your life through coaching, mentoring, or just someone being an accountability partner. Your spouse, if married, can be your accountability partner in one area of your life, and you may have someone else as a coach in another area of your life. Open up your life, let a godly man or woman be praying with you, a professional career coach train you to become your best, or a personal trainer help you get into your best health shape. You need others; that is the bottom line!

The Cost of Conflict

How does conflict come into this? Well, the journey to the best version of yourself is through an inevitable battlefield. I hate to be the bearer of bad news, but you will not really go forward without a fight. You will fight, not physically, but spiritually, psychologically, and emotionally to get where you want to go. You might as well quit right now if you are adamant, you want zero conflict, and yet you want to go forward in your life. You will have to say no to something your flesh requests, and that is a conflict between your flesh and your soul. You might decide, for example, you want to lose twenty pounds and cut back on processed sugar because the doctor said you are pre-diabetic. This journey of losing weight and keeping it off might cost you a bowl of ice cream every night before bedtime or might mean smaller amounts of food portions, regular exercise, or something else. This is conflict because the flesh always wants the easy, comfortable, and hassle-free state.

How about a spiritual goal? Prepare for conflict! Apostle Paul stated,

> *For though we walk in the flesh, we do not war according to the flesh. For the weapons of our warfare are not carnal but mighty in God for pulling down strongholds, casting down arguments and every high thing that exalts itself against the knowledge of God, bringing every thought into captivity to the obedience of Christ.*
>
> **2 Corinthians 10:3–5**

Conflict is inevitable for growth and advancement in life, in every area of your life. You have to have some bulldog tenacity and be willing to fight. Your enemy will sometimes be the man or woman that stares you back in the mirror or may be a demonic spirit that is hell-bent on dragging you to hell through sin, but the common denominator is that you will have to face whatever enemy that stands in your way. Different weapons are needed to face different types of enemies, and you will need to dig in and fight. How would you wear a crown if there was never a conflict? How would you win if there was never a war? How would you be a hero or heroine if there was never hardship? How would you overcome if there was never an obstacle?

❝

If you are typical, you want to avoid conflict at all costs, but if you are wise, you want to arm yourself for every conflict.

I hope you considered the verse above, that though we are in the flesh or have physical bodies, our conflict is not with fellow people. I am not advocating for violence and physical combat with our neighbors or co-workers. We just need to know the nature of our warfare and apply the necessary weapons. So, my friend, I end where I began this chapter: count the cost. Will you pay the cost of convenience, the cost of coaching, and the cost of conflict? If yes, keep reading. If not, keep reading.

CHAPTER SIXTEEN

GATHER THE RESOURCES

So far, the process of going forward has meant you admit you have a problem, decide you want help, and count the cost. To proceed, you now need to gather the resources. You need to design a plan of action. You need to give your desires or dreams some traction. You cannot visualize things in your mind forever. Do not allow yourself to be paralyzed as you try to perfect everything in your mind. This is the stage of organization. You are like a lawyer who has spent a lot of time listening to his client, reading up the law and researching, and then finally sits down with all the materials needed to argue out the case. What is needed to go forward? What is the battle plan? Do I need a trainer, or do I need my spouse to be my accountability partner? How much money is needed to enroll in this weight loss program, or do I even need to sign up for it?

In short, this is the stage where you prepare yourself to take the deep plunge into your best days ahead. You need a roadmap; you need clarity. You need to have the finished product in your mind and the roadmap to get there. You cannot or should not proceed without a plan, and that plan involves putting the resources together. I do not want you to just think finances here; I mean gathering everything you might need in the short term or long term. Gathering resources is really the first step toward starting the journey. Imagine the eve of your wedding night; you will not just be unplanned and unprepared. You are about to enter into marriage and lose the "single" status, and everything you have been doing in the last few weeks is gathering the resources. The man, as someone cleverly observed, is about to "lose his bachelor's degree, and the woman is about to gain her master's degree." The couple typically has been in the process of preparing not just for the wedding but the marriage as well. You prepare for an important interview by reading up about the hiring company, putting your resume together, getting the right attire ready, doing some research on common interview questions and how to answer them, and so on. You must gather the resources.

My wife is guilty of over-packing whenever we are making even short trips. I remember asking her, "Are you relocating?" after I saw the huge bags she had carried for what was supposed to be a short trip. She is good with "gathering the resources" we might need, and often times her wisdom and foresight have served us well during the trips. Look, if you think all this advance preparation is unnecessary, listen to what ants do, "Go to the ant, you sluggard! Consider her ways and be wise, which, having no captain, overseer or ruler, provides her supplies in the summer, *and* gathers her food in the harvest" (Proverbs 6:6–8). The ants use the summer season to gather enough food to eat during winter. They gather resources to help them go forward, so why shouldn't you do the same? I am doing better now, but I used to be notorious for fueling my car when I had literally but fumes in the gas tank. I have been stuck on the highway at least five times when my car has run out of gas. I have no idea why; I just felt the need to see how far I could get with an empty tank. I have since recovered from this addiction to driving with an empty tank; I am going forward!

One simple resource you can get immediately is a journal. Keeping a journal or record of your journey is an excellent self-motivation technique and helps you to reflect and plan better. You can choose to keep a digital journal on your phone or tablet or buy a paper journal to jot down some thoughts with a pen. You might look back many months or years later and see how far you have come in your journey. The resource might also come in handy in helping someone else embark on the same journey you took before. The Lord told Prophet Habakkuk, "Write the vision and make *it* plain on tablets, that he may run who reads it" (Habakkuk 2:2). The prophet was instructed to write plainly what God was unveiling to him so that someone else would use that information in the future. Imagine Apostle Paul never wrote down all the wisdom and revelations God gave him in the course of his ministry! We would not have two-thirds of the New Testament. Enlist those who will be embarking on this journey of going forward with you. Buy the materials you will require. Consult any professional whose services you might require. Best and most important, prepare by far the most important resource, and that is your heart or the mind. You will win or lose the battle in the mind. Now, it is time to get to the next process, and that is to start the journey!

CHAPTER SEVENTEEN
START THE PROCESS

> **Even the best planners have to start at some point. Best plans still need a beginning date, and as simple as it may sound, this is actually a tough part of the journey.**

Putting boots on the ground! We often feel unprepared and under-resourced. We feel a later date is always a better date. We wrongly assume that until every light is green, you cannot leave home. One day I was driving extremely late at night on a rather deserted road, and when I stopped at a red light, a police car pulled beside me. The light stayed red for unusually long, and then the policeman made eye contact with me and then just drove on. I took the cue and then drove on. The road was clear from all directions, and we could not spend the night there because the light was red. The policeman and I knew that, at some point, you have to drive, even through a red light, if safety is observed.

You cannot plan forever. Preparation is particularly important, but execution is just as important. I cannot tell you to start tomorrow, but I can tell you to start at some point, hopefully soon. Perfection happens as we trudge along, making amends and improvements, and you cannot really perfect a process that you never started. For so many years, I wanted to sky-dive, but I was so scared of the actual jumping out of a plane until the day I drove my family to sky-dive in Dallas, about thirty miles from where I live today and actually got into the skydiving class where they brief you on what to do and what to expect. We then boarded the aircraft and lifted up. I was scared, but there was only one way out, the big trap door on the belly of the cargo aircraft. The door was finally opened, and the sound of wind and engine was deafening. The jump, called a tandem jump, meant you were harnessed with an experienced jumper. We were the very last to jump out, and just before we did, I had the unfortunate experience of watching the other guys falling down, in what is called a free fall, at breathtaking speed. Imagine falling down from the sky freely, before the parachute deploys, for sixty seconds. I promise it felt like I fell down for an hour. One minute had never felt so long, but I had to start.

I wanted to conquer the fear of heights. I do not know if it is completely conquered, but who knows, I might actually do this again. My daughter challenged me once to do a tandem jump with her on her eighteenth birthday. Who knows, I might actually consider it! What dad will freak out on a challenge like this from his daughter? The only problem is I know what to expect, which makes it a bit scary. When are you going to start your "better health" project? Put a date that cannot be altered. When are you going back to school for your advanced degree? Call a few places immediately and begin some process. You might not do everything today, but you must not do "nothing" today. You might just need to call a friend to keep you accountable or tell your spouse or pastor. My point is to do something, however infinitesimal, today to mark the start of your journey. Make the deposit today and make the installments gradually!

"Behold, now *is* the accepted time; behold, now *is* the day of salvation" (2 Corinthians 6:2b). Yes, the *now* time is the best time because tomorrow is never guaranteed. We are not asked to finish today but to start today! Pushing the start button may look and mean a different thing to different people, but my urge is for you to push your start button. What does starting look like to you? Do that!

CHAPTER EIGHTEEN

REDIRECT NEGATIVE ENERGY

Many people are struggling to break free from some negative behavior or a destructive cycle and wonder why they keep going back to their old habits.

Momentary seasons of victory will give way to old depressing defeats unless negative energy is replaced with positive energy.

It is not enough to stop doing something bad unless there is an immediate effort to start doing the opposite. Physics teaches us that for every force, there is an opposite and equal force. Shunning the bad is useless unless there is an equal zeal to embrace and practice the good. The Bible teaches us this principle thus, "Do not be overcome by evil, but overcome evil with good" (Romans 12:21).

A good "exit" strategy needs to be accompanied by a good "entry" strategy. We have to work hard to break the negative tendencies through positive replacements. This principle is especially important to avoid seasons of "void" where a negative habit has been broken, but a positive habit of replacing the negative one has not been picked. I have found out that the more I propose not to think about something negative, the more I actually end up thinking about it. The solution is not really to spend time wondering and planning how to avoid negative thoughts but how to start thinking positive thoughts instead. The positive thoughts eventually overshadow the negative thoughts, thus bringing victory. Smoking or alcohol addiction can also be overcome by replacing negative behaviors with positive behaviors, like picking up a sport or learning a new language.

The idea is to ensure that the maximum amount of energy and time is not spent trying to cancel the negative but rather on learning or engaging in a positive.

The more we focus on the negative, the more we reinforce it, but the more we focus on the positive, the more the negative is overshadowed and eventually stifled.

The cure for laziness, for example, is hard work. Judas Iscariot betrayed the Lord and then immediately took his own life. He did not take time to overcome the evil he had done by doing good, which in this case would have been to repent. Peter, on the other hand, denied the Lord but was restored by Jesus and told, "Feed My sheep" (John 21:17).

Peter replaced the negative of denying the Savior by feeding the Savior's sheep. His mission was no longer trying to overcome the shame of his negative actions but the urgency of the mandate to feed the Savior's sheep. The end goal is to engage in the positive, not just keep the negative. Many people pride themselves in the fact that although they are saved, they do not indulge in certain negative behaviors. They imagine they are automatically good just because they do not do what is bad. We do not become good just because we are not doing bad but rather by embracing the one who is the ultimate in goodness, the Lord.

Let me give you some practical tips to help a friend. Do you know anyone spending too much time on the internet watching addictive material like pornography? This evil can be overcome by replacing it with something positive. One can spend the same time watching anointed Gospel music and Christian teaching on the internet instead.

Do you know anyone involved in an illicit extramarital affair? What about helping him/her repent and start an engaging sport like tennis or learn a new language like Mandarin or Spanish? The aim is to replace the negative flow of energy with a positive one. My teacher in middle school used to tell us that an empty mind is the devil's workshop, and this is sensible. We need to exercise faith to overcome fear. Faith is the positive equivalent of the negative emotion of fear. Replacing the negative with the positive will help you go forward.

CHAPTER NINETEEN

CREATE NEW CULTURE

I was trying to help a man who was desperately trying to escape from the strong jaws of alcoholism. He had been a spiritually strong believer some years back, actively involved in church and Christian fellowship. His own wife narrated how the man was so active in evangelism and prayer. The man and his wife then relocated to America, and after a while, he had friends who were always drinking alcohol at social gatherings. The man would attend these parties but would never touch a bottle of wine, though he was constantly teased and ridiculed about it. The man narrated how he had tasted the alcohol once, maybe to prove he could. He did not immediately become addicted, but the mistake he made was not disconnecting himself from the influence of these friends. The passage of time, coupled with the challenges of settling into a new country and culture, was taking a toll on him, and he found himself taking one or two bottles, "social drinking," as it was labeled.

Eventually, the man sank into heavy drinking, leading to stress and family pressure. I sat with him and his wife a few times, trying to help him be delivered and restored from these strong diabolical claws of bondage. He had seasons where he could walk in victory, but he would revert back to seasons of total bondage. The one frustration I had with him initially was his inability or refusal to completely cut off links with his drinking friends. He always maintained that it was no longer the friends who were influencing him to drink since he had the ability to make independent decisions by himself. The Scriptures teach clearly, "Do not be deceived: 'Evil company corrupts good habits'" (1 Corinthians 15:33). You might think you are strong or have a strong will, but you cannot have close friends who have zero influence over you. Prophet Amos asked a question that I want you to answer honestly. The question is this, "Can two walk together, unless they are agreed?" (Amos 3:3). The answer is a big fat no! You are going to influence and get influenced by your close associates. You have to cut ties with those that influence you negatively.

I have had the occasion to talk to the man a few times, and the last conversation I had with him gave me some hope. He had been free from this bondage of alcohol for a while and had been steady in his job. He had not been very keen on his earlier associations, and though I do not have recent updates on his present condition, my hope is that he has forgotten the address of every close friend that is an alcoholic. You have to cut this umbilical cord that feeds you what you are trying to flee from. You must borrow Chevrolet's ad tagline, "find new roads," to escape the clutches of addiction. You have to get out of toxic environments and create a new culture. Why would you spend so much energy and capital trying to fight off temptation in an environment that is full of temptation? Why sit at the table where everyone is drinking freely except you if you really do not want to pick up the habit or are trying to kick it off? Do not try to prove you are so tough; no, my friend, flee to the mountains!

My wife received a bottle of fine wine from her company as a Christmas gift. The bottle was mailed to our house, and my wife wanted to trash it immediately. She asked for my advice, and I advised her to return it with a note thanking them for the gift but declining it on account of her Christian faith. She felt initially like it was rude to send back the gift, and just throwing it into the trash would be enough. We reflected on the issue and concluded that if she did not make her stand well known, they would continue to send wine, whisky, or whatever alcohol to our home as Christmas gifts, and they would never know she did not appreciate it. My wife sent it back. I do not want fine expensive wine coming to my address; who knows, it might come at a time when I am so vulnerable, and I get tempted to just taste a little!

To go forward, find new roads, figuratively, to walk on.

Find new hobbies, new friends, a new job, or simply a new environment. I have no idea exactly what a new culture might look like, but you must find out yourself and adopt it. The beginning point of a new culture will, however, start in your mind because that is where true and effective change begins. "Do not be conformed to this world, but be transformed by the renewing of your mind, that you may prove what *is* that good and acceptable and perfect will of God" (Romans 12:2). Begin to feed your mind with a new diet, and the most nutritious diet is your Bible. That is the one book that will *never* mislead you. That is the one book that has an answer to every human question and problem. Read motivational and inspirational materials, listen to motivational speeches, and listen to godly uplifting music. Spend time with people that inspire and motivate you. Start going to church. Start some beneficial habits, like regular physical exercise, sleeping early and waking up early, and eating healthy. You get my drift; start a new culture!

CHAPTER TWENTY
WALK IN THE SPIRIT

Finally, learn to walk in the Spirit! Walking in the Spirit means to set our minds on the things of God, not on the things of this world. Walking in the Spirit means that our God and His kingdom become our utmost priority so that everything we do is in relation to His kingdom. The opposite of walking in the Spirit is walking in the flesh. Walking in the flesh means setting our minds on the affairs of this world. "For those who live according to the flesh set their minds on the things of the flesh, but those *who live* according to the Spirit, the things of the Spirit" (Romans 8:5).

We can only walk in the Spirit as we surrender our lives to the Lord and allow His Spirit to lead and direct our lives. The Bible declares that it is "'not by might, nor by power, but by My Spirit,' says the LORD of hosts" (Zechariah 4:6b).

Walking in the Spirit means living a life led, directed,

and empowered by the Spirit of the Lord. It means allowing the Lord to govern our lives.

Walking in the flesh means making decisions based on our own experiences, natural wisdom, and human inclinations.

Walking in the flesh leads to a lack of appetite for spiritual things. Prayer and the Word of God become a difficult duty instead of a delightful privilege. Walking in the flesh is dangerous and depressing. We are living in an age where secular humanism, new-age theology, and moral relativism are the order of the day. Traditional Judeo-Christian values have eroded, and as believers in Christ, we must determine to swim upstream against the currents of the world. As someone observed, any dead fish can swim downstream; it takes a living one to swim upstream!

To go forward in our lives and be delivered from anything that has bound us requires walking in the Spirit. We must come to the point of absolute surrender where we set our backs on the world and set our faces to the Lord. We cannot please God unless we walk in the Spirit. The Scriptures declare, "So then, those who are in the flesh cannot please God" (Romans 8:8). Walking in the Spirit is, therefore, the only way to live a life that pleases God and the only way to live a victorious Christian life. Paul states in the Book of Romans, the centerpiece of Christian theology. He says, "For if you live according to the flesh you will die; but if by the Spirit you put to death the deeds of the body, you will live" (Romans 8:13).

How can we start walking in the Spirit today? A short story will illustrate this. Once upon a time, a little mouse was friends with an African elephant. The two animals walked together until they came to a big bridge, which the little mouse was scared to cross. The elephant asked the mouse to hop onto his large ear, and the two crossed safely over. The large bridge shook and creaked under the weight of the elephant. Once on the other side, the little mouse declared, "Wow, Elephant, we really shook that bridge, didn't we?" You and I are like that small mouse. We cannot shake the bridge of life by ourselves. When we allow the Lord to carry us through, we will shake the kingdom of darkness.

David declared to the Lord, "For by You I can run against a troop, by my God I can leap over a wall" (Psalm 18:29). Victorious Christian life is swimming upstream. It is turning away from the world, the flesh, and the devil. We cannot be friends with the world and friends with God at the same time. Friendship with the world means loving and being governed by the principles of the world, disregarding the parameters set by the Word of God. The Scriptures solemnly warn those who care to listen, "Do you not know that friendship with the world is enmity with God? Whoever therefore wants to be a friend of the world makes himself an enemy of God" (James 4:4b).

I do not know what you have been thinking as you read this book. My prayer is that you will be challenged to go forward and not allow the limitation or mistakes of yesterday to hold you back. God's plan for your life is to arise and shine. His grace is sufficient to heal the mistakes and sins of your past and present life. You can arise, go forward, and help others go forward tomorrow. It is never too late. Along with you, I want to believe that God will deliver you from any past issues holding you back. Your past failure or even success should not block your vision for tomorrow. Your life can have a happy, victorious ending. Stop whatever else you are doing and pray with me right now. Use this prayer of mine while you exercise your faith.

Say, "Lord, I come to You in the precious name of Your Son, Jesus Christ. I realize that my life is stuck, and You are the only One strong enough to set me free. I come to You in faith and ask You to set me free right now. I confess, and I repent every sin in my life and ask for forgiveness. Help and empower me with Your blessed Holy Spirit to live a life that is victorious and that honors You. By faith, I am free, and I am going forward in Jesus' mighty name. Amen."

Go forward!

ABOUT THE AUTHOR

Patrick Kariuki, born in Kenya, is a resident of Dallas, Texas. He holds a bachelor of arts degree in social work from the University of Nairobi and a master of arts degree in Christian education from Mid-America Baptist Theological Seminary in Cordova, Tennessee. Patrick is the pastor of Renewal Springs Church in Dallas, Texas.

Patrick is married to Miriam, and they are blessed with two teenagers, Bill and Jill.

To reach out to Patrick, email renewalsprings@gmail.com

Printed in the USA
CPSIA information can be obtained
at www.ICGtesting.com
LVHW021316121123
763661LV00102B/5004

9 798887 386010